Princesses, Dragons and Helicopter Stories

Helicopter Stories is tried, tested and proven to have a significant impact on children's literacy and communication skills, their confidence and social and emotional development. Based on the work of Vivian Gussin Paley, this book provides a practical, step-by-step guide to using this approach with young children.

Covering all aspects of Helicopter Stories, Trisha Lee shows you how you can introduce the approach to children for the first time, collect their stories and then bring their ideas to life by acting them out. Full of anecdotes and practical examples from a wide range of settings, the book includes:

- Clear guidelines and rules for scribing children's stories, and acting them out
- How to deal with taboos and sensitive issues in children's stories
- How to involve children who are unwilling to speak or act
- Supporting children with English as an Additional Language
- Links to show how the approach supports children's holistic development.

Providing an accessible guide to an approach that is gaining international recognition and featuring a foreword by Vivian Gussin Paley, this book will be essential reading for all those who want to support children's learning in a way that is fun, engaging and proven to work.

Trisha Lee is a professionally trained theatre director, with a wide range of practical and academic skills. She is passionate about the importance of storytelling and drama in children's lives, particularly in the early years. In 2002 Trisha founded MakeBelieve Arts, a theatre and education company offering innovative, high-quality theatre and education programmes to develop the creative potential of children aged 2–15.

Vivian Gussin Paley is a retired kindergarten teacher from the University of Chicago Laboratory School. She has published numerous books about her work, and has received many awards, including being named Outstanding Educator by the National Council of Teachers of English in 2004.

Princesses, Dragons and Helicopter Stories

Storytelling and Story Acting in the early years

Trisha Lee

Routledge
Taylor & Francis Group

LONDON AND NEW YORK

First published 2016
by Routledge
2 Park Square, Milton Park, Abingdon, Oxon OX14 4RN

and by Routledge
711 Third Avenue, New York, NY 10017

Routledge is an imprint of the Taylor & Francis Group, an informa business

British Library Cataloguing in Publication Data
A catalogue record for this book is available from the British Library

Library of Congress Cataloging-in-Publication Data
Lee, Trisha.
  Princesses, dragons and helicopter stories : storytelling and story acting in the early years / Trisha Lee.
    pages cm
  Includes bibliographical references and index.
  1. Storytelling—Study and teaching. I. Title.
   LB1042.L 43 2016
   372.67'7044—dc23
   2015011527

ISBN: 978-1-138-79764-2 (hbk)
ISBN: 978-1-138-79765-9 (pbk)
ISBN: 978-1-315-75696-7 (ebk)

Typeset in Galliard
by Apex CoVantage, LLC

To Bill and Callum, for filling my life with stories . . .

Contents

Foreword

Trisha Lee plays a magical role in classrooms all over the world. With only pen, paper and masking tape in hand, she can turn any group of children into an acting company. The children become storytellers, actors, and audience, and their teachers emerge as scribes, narrators and stage managers: the classroom is transformed into the make-believe worlds that children love best.

For those of us who worry that technology is stealing away the magic of childhood, Ms. Lee's captivating and instructive book will bring relief and pleasure. She shows us that it is still the children's own imaginations that unlock their unique identities and poetic natures. The words come from the children, and every expression grows in meaning and richness when reimagined inside a script and acted out with classmates. The power of fantasy to enhance language and build community is inescapable. Trisha Lee takes us through the process, step by step, with skill and enthusiasm.

We humans are born knowing how to place our thoughts and images into stories. Even the shyest three-year-old is eager to dictate a story if it will be acted out in the company of classmates. How fortunate that an early childhood classroom is populated by such a variety of characters, enough different types to satisfy all our dreams. Our superheroes and baby bears, our mommies, dinosaurs and runaway kittens are just waiting to be invited to step on to the stage.

The child says, in effect: If you let me pretend to be what I want to be while everyone watches and listens to me, I will give you my story and listen to yours. To which the teacher adds: If you and your classmates will act out your stories together, we will help one another reveal who we are and who we want to become, in a kinder, more generous and thoughtful classroom community.

And yet, haven't our pretend superheroes been rescuing mommies and baby bears from monsters all along, and without the teacher's help? Is it really so different when these developing plots and characters are dictated, written down and acted out on a space marked off with masking tape? This is one of the many questions answered for us in *Princesses, Dragons and Helicopter Stories* while we are being entertained and inspired.

Trisha Lee is a persuasive dramatist. Her admiration and respect for the lyrical imaginations of her young storytellers and actors make me want to return to a kindergarten classroom and take my place once again in the theatre of the young.

Vivian Gussin Paley
Chicago, Illinois

Vivian Gussin Paley is a retired kindergarten teacher from the University of Chicago Laboratory School. She has published numerous books about her work. In 1989 she received a MacArthur Fellowship, in 1987 the Erikson Award for Service to Children, in 1998 a

Lifetime Achievement American Book Award from the Before Columbus Foundation and the John Dewey Society's Outstanding Achievement Award in 2000. In 2004, she was named Outstanding Educator by the National Council of Teachers of English.

For more than 15 years Trisha Lee has worked with Vivian Gussin Paley's Storytelling and Story Acting curriculum. Through MakeBelieve Arts, she and her colleague Isla Hill have designed a programme of professional development based upon this approach.

This has come to be known as Helicopter Stories.

In 2013 Helicopter Stories was evaluated by the Open University. Since that time MakeBelieve Arts has established Centres of Excellence across the UK and offers Helicopter Starter and Helicopter Practitioner training.

In the pages that follow, Trisha Lee explores how stories and fantasy play engage all young children and help them to draw connections and make sense of the world.

Introduction
The girl with pigtails

Imagine a girl with pigtails, sat at a desk, in a school in Gloucestershire. The year is 1975, and the girl is bored. She fidgets, she chats to her mates and eventually she is sent out of the room. Years go by and the pattern repeats: more wriggling, more talking, more empty-corridors punishments, except in one class. In one class she is never sent out; in one class she never has to be reminded to pay attention; in one class she finds Utopia.

The lesson is drama; the girl is me.

School failed me. I was the child who spent more time in the corridor than I ever did in the classroom. If you asked my teachers about my crime, each would give you the same list; I was a fidget who couldn't sit still; I talked too much and never listened; only in drama did I excel.

Needless to say, I left school at 16, with very few qualifications and a passion for theatre. Too young to apply for drama school, I set up a theatre company and began touring a show to youth clubs about youth unemployment. I funded this company on my dole money, charged £5 for groups of young people to watch it and made a profit. However, in my school's eyes, I was the girl who failed.

At the age of 19, with no A levels and equipped only with determination and my refusal to take no for an answer, I managed to get a place at Dartington College of Arts and began studying towards a degree in theatre.

As a result of exploring the one thing I loved, I opened myself up to learning. I realised that, despite what my teachers had said, I did have a brain and I could sit still to study, as long as the work in front of me made me excited.

Years later, I found out about multiple intelligences, and I discovered that I wasn't a fidget; I was a kinaesthetic learner. I needed to move to think. My teachers were probably right, I did talk too much, but I had highly developed interpersonal skills. I cared about the people in my class and wanted to know about their lives and solve problems with them. School spent so much time criticising me for my learning style that it failed to see the strengths that these skills gave me.

At drama school, because I was energised, I was fully engaged. I no longer became easily distracted. My neurons were firing, so I worked long hours to catch up with my classmates. I wanted to be 'clever' enough to understand this subject that fed my passion.

I was in an environment where I could take risks. I tried out different roles. I made up stories, acted in a wide range of situations, used symbolism, metaphor and make believe to explore social relations through the medium of pretend play. Plus, I had the luxury of doing this five days a week for four years.

Don't let anyone tell you any differently – drama school is the kindergarten of adults, and it was through this form of education, that I entered my twenties, with a drive to reengage with learning.

Choose a job you love, and you will never have to work a day in your life.

(Confucius)

I left college in 1988 and began working in theatre and education. I was lucky enough to uncover my inner passion, or as Ken Robinson (2009) calls it, I found my 'element'. I became fascinated in how children learn, and I wanted to find out why education had failed me. I began to make links between the theatre work I loved and the fantasy play of the children I worked with. I knew there was a connection, but it took me a long time to understand it.

And then in 1999 I came across the work of Vivian Gussin Paley, and finally it began to make sense.

This book shares some of the stories that I, and many of the people I've worked with, have uncovered over the past 15 years that have led me to become an advocate for Vivian Gussin Paley's Storytelling and Story Acting curriculum, as a foundation for children's development in the early years.

The first section is a step-by-step guide that I have developed to support practitioners in delivering regular Storytelling and Story Acting sessions in their settings.

The second section examines the child-centred philosophy that underpins this approach.

At MakeBelieve Arts we call this work Helicopter Stories, after Vivian Gussin Paley's book *The Boy Who Would Be a Helicopter* (1990). There are many other names for Storytelling and Story Acting that have been adopted around the world. I have heard it called Story Square, Story Play, Doing Stories, Dragonfly, the Storytelling Curriculum, Carpet Drama, Magic Carpet and numerous other titles.

Whatever you name it, I believe that if you use it on a regular basis with a group of children, you will find yourself in the incredible position of letting imagination fly.

Figure I.1 Helicopter Stories

Section I

The how

Helicopter Stories: The four stages of introduction

The classroom that does not create its own legends has not travelled beneath the surface to where the living takes place.

(Vivian Gussin Paley 1990)

1 A sense of anticipation
Introducing Story Acting

There were five spiders; they were climbing up their web.
Suddenly it went dark and there was lightning and it was swirling around.
And all the spiders were frightened and ran back into their house.
And it was a monster, stamping his feet and making a noise.

(Nathan, age 4)

When we enter the theatre for the first time, walk to our seats and sit down, something dormant inside us comes alive. We have anticipation about what we are going to watch. The location shapes our expectations. This is true whether it is a West End theatre, a small blacked-out room on the top floor of a public house or even a dusty village hall. Sometimes we see the stage laid out with props or furniture for the first scene. Sometimes it is empty or curtained, hiding from us its secrets. Whatever the situation, the thrill of people coming together to form an audience and the fact that we are sat facing the area where the story will unfold empower the stage, bestowing on it a sense of mystery.

When I enter a new classroom and share Helicopter Stories for the first time, I also have this sense of anticipation. The children are not aware of what we are going to do as I gather them together on the carpet, but I can feel their curiosity as we hold hands, make a circle and sit down. Looking around the room at the line of expectant faces, I wonder what stories I will uncover. I am keen to see how the children will act them out and what marvels they will reveal to me.

I am never disappointed.

The class room has all the elements of the theatre, and the observant, self-examining teacher will not need a drama critic to uncover character and plot, and meaning. We are, all of us, the actors trying to find the meaning of the scenes in which we find ourselves.

The scripts are not yet fully written, so we must listen with curiosity and great care to the main characters who are, of course, the children.

(Paley 1986)

I find listening with 'curiosity and great care' the most exciting aspect of this work. We are engaged on a journey. It is improvisation, and neither I nor the children know where the stories will take us.

A simple approach

Helicopter Stories is in theory a simple approach. The practitioner sits with the child, listens to their story, and writes it down word for word. Once the story is finished, the child decides which character they would like to play and the scribe takes a story from the next on the list.

Towards the end of the session, the class gather together, ready to observe and take part in the stories of their peers. A simple stage is marked on the floor and the classroom is transformed into a theatre.

As the children prepare to act out their stories, the classroom is filled with the quiet of an expectant audience, waiting to see what happens when the curtains rise. The first phrase of the first story is read, the theatre begins, and the children in turn leave their places around the stage, to become princesses or superheroes, helicopters or dragons, babies or mummies. When the narrative ends, the children who remained seated clap thank you, and the stage is cleared, ready for the next tale, and the new cast to emerge.

During Story Acting, each child takes on several responsibilities. At times they are audience, watching spellbound as their classmates perform. Moments later they are actors, creating the trees in the magical forest, or the baby who lost his mum, or the baddy that fought Batman. Then they are the storyteller, able to cast themselves as the character they've always wanted to be.

Introducing Helicopter Stories is a speedy process. In this chapter I explore the first stage of this approach:

Stage one

Assemble the group, hold hands in a large circle and sit down. The space should be big enough for everyone to sit comfortably, and it must contain room for a stage in the middle.

It is vital that everyone has a front row seat. This is theatre in the round, but it is also participatory theatre. Each child should be able to stand up and step onto the stage without having to climb over their peers.

Creating the stage

As soon as everyone is together, we are ready to begin.

This is a community event. Where possible, ensure all the adults are present. This gives a value that might not be there if some members of staff are preparing for the next activity.

We start by marking a masking-tape stage. Normally this is a rectangle, but sometimes the size of the room or the way people sit makes for wigglier lines. None of this matters. The only thing that counts is that everyone fit around the edges and that there be plenty of space inside for acting.

Leaving the stage down

Once the stage is established, it is possible to leave it down and re-mark it only when it begins to age. Alternatively you may choose to take it up at the end of every session and re-create it each time that it's needed. This could be done as a ritual in front of the children or as preparation before they arrive.

My preference is always to leave the stage down. Whenever I do, the children make use of it. I have seen groups, uninstructed, sitting around the edges, leading the acting out with their peers or playing Helicopter Stories in the centre.

Sometimes the practical issue of flooring makes this impossible.

Note to myself

If you leave a masking-taped stage down on a parquet floor, it tends to leave a mark, as it pulls the varnish off.

Leaving tape down on a deep-pile carpet creates a sticky mess when you unpeel it.

Both these examples come from experience and a lot of apologising.

If I had my own classroom, I'd paint a white square on the floor, making Helicopter Stories a permanent feature of the room.

Different types of stage

I have seen various other ways to delineate a stage.

In one school in the United States, the teacher created a tie-dye sheet with the help of the children. This was laid on the floor at each Story Acting session. Although the cloth rucked up whilst the children were acting, the five-year-olds coped perfectly.

Coming from a theatre background, I have been trained not to let anyone walk, let alone run, spin or act on any floor cloth unless it is pulled taut and then gaffer taped down on all sides by a qualified stage manager. The group hadn't had this training and ignored my health and safety wincing as they slid and wriggled over it. Children have an ability to cope and make do with most things, but as I watched the cloth wrap around their ankles, I longed to give them the freedom of a carpeted floor.

Another option is to use a mat to signify the stage area. Sometimes this is too small and slips while the children move. Sometimes it is primary coloured and feels louder than the acting out. Sometimes this is a quick and efficient solution.

My preference will always be masking tape. Thank goodness, the children are more concerned with the important things, like telling their stories and having them acted out.

Ritual openings

Practitioners sometimes develop ritualistic ways of opening Storytelling and Story Acting. One teacher lit a joss stick and chimed a bell at the start of each session. Another invited everyone to pat the stage once the tape was in place. My favourite example was shared with me by my colleague Isla Hill. It came from a reception classroom in London.

The children sat around the taped out square and closed their eyes.

'When you open your eyes, in front of you will be our stage, and you will be transported to the theatre', said their teacher.

These rituals are not part of what I define as 'the process'. They are the individual sparks that each of us bring to the work. They ensure that the gift Vivian Gussin Paley gives us is taken and owned by everyone who connects with her approach.

Magical qualities of a stage

One afternoon, in a school in Westminster, Jamal, a reception-age child whose class I was working with, was playing in the nursery. At the same time, Isla Hill was taking stories from the nursery children. Although I had worked with Jamal's class in the morning, he asked Isla if she would take a story from him. She apologised and told him that she only took stories from the younger children.

Jamal stopped, deep in thought. He turned to Isla and said,

'Have the nursery got a stage?'

Isla told him the stage had been down all week and asked if he'd not noticed it. He hadn't. His next question was more urgent.

'Where is the stage? Can I see it?'

Isla took Jamal to an area of the nursery that was covered by a large rectangular shape made of masking tape, left over from the previous week. It was exactly like the one in his classroom.

Jamal stared for the longest of time and then, acknowledging the power that stages have had throughout the centuries, he bent down, touched the tape with his hand, nodded and ran off.

This five-year-old boy bestowed magical qualities on the stage. He was reverent in the way he approached it. Describing his actions afterwards, Isla said that a quietness came over him, and she sensed his feelings of awe and his awareness that this was the place where stories could happen.

Whatever his thoughts, they stayed with him, and a week later, when I next entered his classroom, he ran to me and almost conspiratorially, as if he were disclosing a great secret, he whispered in my ear,

'The nursery have a stage too'.

I smiled at him, and for an instant we shared this mystery.

Beginning the process of acting out

Throughout this book, at the top of each chapter and dotted around inside of it, are stories I use to introduce the approach to a new group. All of these were dictated by children aged three to seven.

If you'd like to use other stories, the best ones contain only a few characters and have clear moments of action. This ensures that the first session is not over complicated.

Tell the group that the story you are about to share with them was created by another child. Ask them to help bring it to life.

First stories

Read the first sentence of the first story. Moving in order around the group, invite children to act out the various roles.

Once the opening characters are on the stage, read the next line and bring in the next set of actors, pacing the story, to give children time to respond to the narrative.

A transcript of an introductory session

Hello, I've got some stories I'd like to share with you, they were told to me by some other children in a different setting. They are from 4 year olds. I wondered if you would be interested in acting them out. Let me read you the first story.

(Read) **A little puppy saw a flower.**

In fact, let's start there. (Indicating to a child in the circle.) *Can you pretend to be a puppy? Will you come up onto the stage? How does the puppy walk around? Can you show me?*

(Indicating the next child in the circle) *Would you be the flower? Can you stand up and come onto the stage? How could you make yourself look like a flower?*

(Read) **The puppy smelt the flower.**

(Asking the child playing the puppy) *Can I see you smell the flower?*

(Read) **And he saw a tree.**

(Inviting the next child in the circle to come onto the stage) *Will you come and be the tree? I'm curious to see how you will do it? Fantastic!*

(Read) **The puppy walked all the way around the tree, until his mother came to find him.**

(Again indicating to the next child around the stage) *Would you be the mother dog coming to find him? How does the mother dog walk? Can I see you looking for your baby? Can you find him? Excellent! And that is the end of the first story. Shall we clap thank you?*
(All the children in the first story sit down again where they came from.)
Do you want to hear another story?

(Read) **One day three skipping Turtles.**

(Carrying on from where we are in the circle, counting the children onto the stage) *One, two, three, can you three pretend to be skipping Turtles. How do you think Turtles skip? Can I see your turtles skipping around the stage?*

(Read) **And the Butterfly says, 'Turtles don't skip'.**

(Pointing to the next child in the circle) *Let's see; can you be the Butterfly? Can I see you flying around the stage?*
(Asking all the children around the stage) *Shall we all say 'Turtles don't skip'?*

(Read) **Then a deer says, 'If you skip, you can't be a Turtle'.**

(Next child invited up) *Will you play the Deer? I wonder how a Deer moves. Can you show me?*
(Talking to the class) *Shall we all say the words? 'If you skip, you can't be a Turtle'.*

(Read) **But they keep skipping and they keep being skippers, because some Turtles can skip.**

(To the whole class) *Let's clap thank you. Would you like to do another one?*

(Read) **There were five spiders.**

(Pointing to the next five children around the stage) *One, two, three, four, five, will you come and be the spiders? Can you show me how the spiders crawl around the stage?*

(Read) **They were climbing up their web.**

(To the spiders) *Can I see you climbing up your web?*

(Read) **Suddenly it went dark and there was lightning, and it was swirling around.**

(Counting to bring children onto the stage) *One, two, will you come and be the lightning? How does the lightning move? Can you show me? Can I see the lightning swirling around?*

(Read) **And all the spiders were frightened and ran back into their house.**

(Speaking to the spiders) *Can I see the spiders looking frightened and running back to their house?*

(Read) **And it was a monster, stamping his feet and making a noise.**

(Speaking to the lightning) *Let me see the lightning becoming a monster, stamping its feet and making a noise.*

(To the whole class) **Brilliant, and that's the end of the story. Let's clap thank you.**

Now, I wonder if anyone would like to tell me a story. (In Chapter 2, I describe this next step, scribing a story across the stage.)

Clapping thank you

At the end of each story, ask the children to clap thank you to the storyteller and the story actors. This reinforces the role of the audience and shows appreciation for the work.

In some settings children take a bow before sitting down. If the group introduces this, I go along with it; if not, we clap, and the actors return to their places around the stage.

In one class, the group developed different ways of applauding. In a video posted on the Boston Listens website, the teacher asked the children what chicken applause looked like, and the class moved their arms like chickens whilst making animal noises. She then guided them through a range of different types of applause, from silent applause to loud applause to leg applause made by clapping their feet together. The children took ownership of the idea and started to invent their own applause, including head applause, created by shaking your head vigorously, and robot applause, where your arms move up and down like robots. The playfulness of this class was encouraged and resulted in its incorporation of this ritual after each story was acted out.

A giant step

Place this three year old in a room with other threes, and sooner or later they will become an acting company.

Should there happen to be a number of somewhat older peers about to offer stage directions and dialogue, the metamorphosis will come sooner rather than later.

The dramatic images that flutter about through their minds as so many unbound streams of consciousness, novels begin to emerge as audible scripts to be performed on demand.

(Paley 1990)

Stepping onto a stage for the first time can be a giant step for a child or an adult. The act of standing up, moving forward and walking into the unknown should not be underestimated. For some children it can be a major event in developing their confidence.

Leading Story Acting comes with responsibilities. As a facilitator, it is my role to look after everyone I invite onto the stage, regardless of their age. If they are not ready for it or if they shake their heads when it is their turn, I acknowledge their decision, recognise they still have a role as a story listener and don't try to force them.

When children first start acting, they often face the person who is reading the story, sometimes standing very close to them in a long line. Often in these early sessions, children will perform all their actions in one direction, as if afraid to take further steps.

In the next sections are some suggestions that might get children moving.

Asking, not showing

When children enter the stage, I invite them to demonstrate the way their character moves. I do this by asking questions: 'Can I see how the puppy crawls around the stage?'

By adding the words 'around the stage', I open up the space to them, suggesting they can move around. For many children this subtle use of language works. Suddenly they become a puppy crawling across the space.

The process of acting is something children do every day, whether in the dolls corner or in the blocks, they are continually taking on characters and creating stories. The only difference with Story Acting is they are doing it in front of an audience.

Less confident children

There are children who will stand still during those early acting days. We don't need to pressure them. They have already taken an enormous journey by entering the stage. Experience shows me that as children relax, they find freedom in acting their stories. The less I push them, the more self-assured they become. Some children take longer than others. This is fine.

Inviting a friend

If a child wants to be involved but looks nervous about playing a character on his own, I may ask for two lions or three fairies. This allows children to act with their peers. We all feel more confident when we're with a friend.

Once upon a time there was a walking shoe, and the shoe decided to go for a swim. And he sunk. Then he said, 'Maybe I should buy a rubber ring?'

And then there was a little girl who said, 'You can borrow my rubber ring'.

(Sandi, age 5)

When I asked Eddie to take on the role of the 'walking shoe', he shook his head. He was sat next to Jamie, who was much more confident. I invited the two of them to play the shoe. They curled up together and shuffled across the stage in unison, much to the delight of the audience. Eddie would not have been able to do this on his own, but working with Jamie gave him the support he needed.

If the story belongs to a child who is in the room, I check that she is happy to have more than one child playing the character. The children mostly agree; this is the kind of negotiation that they are used to during play.

MICHAEL: I want to be the lion.
JAMIE: I want to be the lion.
MICHAEL: Okay, let's have two lions . . .

If a child is anxious about getting something wrong, ask the storyteller to demonstrate the character.

Being curious

I am curious to know how the lion moves – could you show me?

The phrase 'I am curious' can alleviate the pressure on a child who wants to get it right. Now he is being asked to share his way of doing it.

Asking for verbs

If children won't move, think of questions you could ask to encourage them to take risks. Asking for verbs work best.

Can I see how the Princess walks around the stage?
Can you show me how Spiderman shoots his web?
Can I see the lion crawling through the jungle?

Here are some other phrases that might help.

Can you show me what game the children are playing?
I'm curious, how would you pretend to be a house?
Can I see how the mummy packs her suitcase?
Could I hear the baby crying?
Shall we all pretend to be the baby crying?

Although I ask children how their character moves, I never physically demonstrate what an action might look like.

Try doing it like this

By the time we are adults, we have acquired a selection of standard movements. If someone asks us to cook, we may imagine a saucepan and begin to stir; throwing a ball may consist of an overarm pitch.

When working with children, it is easy to demonstrate an action in a bid to encourage them to respond, but if we watch and wait, the movements we see are often surprising.

If you catch yourself demonstrating and realise it is a habit you find hard to break, try sitting on your hands during Story Acting and see what the children do without your help. Monitor the difference between this and what happens when you show them how to act.

The tiniest of movements

When I first started delivering Helicopter Stories, we always had two people working together, one to lead the session and one to note the other, writing down exactly what they said and did so that later we could discuss what happened.

We realised that when we led the acting out, we demonstrated to the children how we thought they should move. One day we decided to sit on our hands.

I was the first to have a go at this new approach. The girl whose story I was working on was three-year-old Miranda. She was painfully shy, and this was her first story. It was very short.

'I playing with a ball.'

I sat on my hands and invited her onto the stage. She stood facing me, inches from my leg. I asked her to show me how she played with the ball. She looked at me. I looked at her. I was itching to demonstrate throwing a ball into the air, but I didn't move. I looked at her again. Then I really looked at her. Her hands were cupped together, I hadn't noticed it before. Her fingers were moving, ever so gently, up and down, as if lightly throwing a ball into the air and then catching it again. It was the tiniest of movements, so easy to miss, but as soon as I saw it, I knew what she was doing.

'Is that your ball?' I asked.

Miranda nodded. I placed my hands in the same way as her and began to mirror her actions. I showed the rest of the class, inviting them to join in. They copied Miranda. A smile appeared on her face and she threw her ball a little bit harder.

People as objects

If a story contains an object or building, try to incorporate it into the acting out, inviting one or two children to make the shape of it with their bodies. If there is a castle, ask the storyteller to help the actors create it.

It's important not to clutter the story with objects, but if there is something that grabs your imagination or feels important, then ask the storyteller if she would like someone to play it. Don't impose a way of creating this shape onto the children. It's more rewarding to let them solve the problem themselves.

When you ask a child to represent an object, think beforehand about what you are inviting her to do. Asking her to make a house is a clear instruction. Asking her to show you how to 'be a park' is more abstract.

If I wanted to bring a park to life, I'd be more specific. I'd bring trees in, or the swings, rather than asking someone to represent the whole location. However, there is no need to create the landscape of a park if the trees, swings or slides are not mentioned in the story.

If you check with the storyteller about whether she'd like someone to become one of the objects, this is less likely to happen.

This is the child's world. We do not need to people it with our own imagination.

Sound effects

If a story has any elements that inspire sound effects, then the children will enjoy making these. If a wind is blowing, ask the storyteller what the wind sounds like, or involve the audience in creating a soundscape.

Stories with dialogue

Where there is a line of dialogue, ask the character to speak it. If he is reluctant, invite the whole class to say the words together. If the story suggests words that haven't been written, ask the storyteller if the character says anything.

Pretend

When I lead Story Acting I use the word 'pretend' a lot.

Pretend you are riding on the horse.

Pretend you are sitting on the toadstool.

Children are fluent in the language of pretend. I don't need to explain it. Pretend is the currency of their everyday existence. This word has the power to stop them *really* sitting on the horse and squashing the child or climbing up their friend who is pretending to be the tree. Pretend is the vocabulary of acting. We know it's not real; we're just making up how it might be.

Maximum numbers

I am often asked what the optimum number is for Helicopter Stories. I don't think there is any right answer. I have led sessions with small groups of children as part of their key groups, as well as working with whole classes. In one setting of three- to four-year-olds, I worked with forty children in one go.

As long as there is room for all the children to have a front row seat, then Storytelling and Story Acting works. With a small group, participants have the chance to tell and take part in more stories; with the whole class there is the opportunity to develop a sense of community in the classroom.

Working with large numbers is always my preference, and if there is a mixed age group of children the session becomes even richer.

Being surprised

Four-year-old Diego spoke very little English. One day he told me a story about a dinosaur.

'Dinosaur, roar!'

When I asked if he could show me how the dinosaur moved, he looked quizzically at me, then moulded both his fingers so that only three were visible on each hand. He made a scratching motion in front of him. It surprised me. Here was a boy who spoke very little English, showing me exactly how a Tyrannosaurus moved. His gestures were intricate.

Realising I'd been taken off guard, I questioned myself. Perhaps I had expected a more stereotypical representation of a dinosaur, a roaring, charging dinosaur. But this four-year-old knew about dinosaurs. He didn't go for a cheap stereotype. When I asked him to show me how a dinosaur moved, he looked at me as if to say, 'What type of dinosaur would you like to see, a Stegosaurus, a Diplodocus?' Not getting a suitable response, he opted for his own personal favourite, the Tyrannosaurus.

By observing the way children represent characters or objects, we slice a window into their world, and we learn loads about dinosaurs.

Always be prepared to be surprised.

Introducing Story Acting – summary of points

- Ensure the children have room to sit comfortably around a taped-out stage.
- Introduce the approach using stories from other children or ones you have created yourself.
- Read stories one sentence at a time, and then invite children onto the stage to act out each sequence.
- Select children in order, moving around the stage to ensure everyone has a turn.
- Use verbs to encourage children to demonstrate the actions of a character.
- Clap thank you at the end of each story.
- You can leave the stage down to allow for children to continue to play at acting out stories, but this can result in a sticky residue on the floor.
- Remember that stepping onto the stage for the first time can be scary.
- Allow two or more children to play one character.
- Accept that some children might not move when they first come onto the stage.
- Do not demonstrate how a character should be represented; ask questions instead.
- Watch for small gestures that you might normally miss.
- Have people play objects as well as characters.
- Don't ask children to be locations that are abstract, such as a park.
- Incorporate sound effects into a story.
- If stories contain dialogue, invite the actor or the whole class to speak the words.
- The word 'pretend' can help to ensure children play at riding a horse rather than squashing the friend.
- The number of children in a group should accommodate your needs; there are no optimum sizes.
- Be prepared to be surprised.

2 Would anyone like to tell me a story?

Scribing a story around the stage

Once upon a time there was a ballerina dancing in her dance class.
Then a dragon come and breathe fire out in the dance class.
The dragon breathe fire on the ballerina. Then the Ballerina said,
'Help, help'. Then her go into her house and her can't see anymore the dragon.
Then she go back to her dance class, safe.

(Alicia, age 5)

As soon as everyone has acted in a few stories the children are ready to dictate their own. I introduce this with the following question:

'Who wants to tell a story for us to act?'

When I ask this question to a room of two- to five-year-olds, I am greeted by a sea of hands. They are keen to participate, even though they have no idea how it will work. I am amazed at the trust that children place in adults when faced with new experiences. Their hands shoot up and their faces eagerly announce, 'Yes, I will have a go, even though I don't know what having a go involves'.

When I ask the same question to a room of adults, I find myself surrounded by people who discover that their shoes have become the most interesting objects in the world. It's astonishing how the bravery we have as children dissipates as we get older, only to be replaced by a variety of ostrich-like tactics. 'If I stare at my feet and don't look at the workshop leader, maybe she won't see me?'

Perhaps as children we gave our trust to too many adults, only to find ourselves feeling embarrassed when the rules weren't clear or we became the butt of the joke. Maybe we taught ourselves to shut down, hoping someone else would step forward so that we could see how they were treated before we took the risk ourselves.

The more I see how hard it is for adults to step into the unknown, the more clarity I have that our job is to protect the children we work with, to make the stage and Storytelling and Story Acting a secure place, where all their words and actions are valued. Helicopter Stories has to be an activity where children can take risks and don't feel humiliated or unsafe.

Scribing stories around the stage

Taking one or two stories around the stage enables all the children to see firsthand exactly what the process involves. After this introduction, scribing takes place as Private Stories (see Chapter 3.)

Once a child volunteers to tell a story, I ask her to sit next to me. Some people invite the child to tell the story from where she is, but I like to bring her closer, for two reasons;

first, so I can hear accurately what she is saying, and second, so that while I am writing, she can see the paper and, if she is interested, watch me capturing her words. Often I join the children on the stage if they are reluctant to come too close.

The story book

As the children speak their story, I write their words in an A5 book. This size ensures that children have enough space for their ideas but also that stories are not too long to act out.

The type of book is down to the individual.

Some people use beautiful journals, believing they give a sense of prestige to the children's words. This is probably more for you than for the children, who are equally happy to dictate their stories onto scraps of paper.

One class I worked with gave a book to all the children, so that all their stories were kept together in one place. This provided the class teacher with a record of progression, and it meant that the children could share their stories with their parents, carrying them from home to school in their book bags.

I have known people to use triplicate carbon books, enabling them to keep one, place one in the child's records and send one home. For a while at MakeBelieve Arts we used duplicate books, which allowed us to keep a copy but also to hand over the original at the end of each session. The disadvantage of this was that some of the copies were hard to read.

I have met practitioners who type up the stories after each workshop. This can become a laborious task, and it would be a tragedy if this made Storytelling and Story Acting seem like a chore.

The way the teacher presents the stories to the world is probably irrelevant to the child. Weigh up the adult need to demonstrate or justify the approach (often important within the current educational climate) with the quantity and workload such a task demands.

Over the years I've created books out of folded A4 paper, used A5 exercise pads and produced attractively crafted binders. None of these has had an impact on the engagement of the children or the stories they produce.

Each story should be no longer than one A5 page

As children get familiar with the approach, their stories get longer. The one-A5-page-per-story rule ensures that no story is too long and that there is time for them all to be acted out on the day they are taken.

After writing the child's name in the top right hand corner of the page, I say the following sentence: 'This is your page. I've put your name at the top. Now your story can be as short as you like, but it cannot be any longer than the bottom of this page'.

This wording has become my script. I have tried other variations, but I realised it is easy to accidently put the emphasis on a story needing to be as long as the page or to tell the children that their stories have to be short. The suggested sentence is a nonjudgemental way to define the boundaries.

If, when they reach the bottom of the page, the child still has more story, I tell him that he can add to it next time, like another chapter in a book.

Angeline was five years old when she told her version of *Goldilocks and the Three Bears* over a period of four weeks. Each time I visited her classroom, she asked if she could continue her story. Before I started scribing, I read her the extract from the week before. She then dictated the next section, crafting the tale until the page was full. When we acted out each chapter, I reread the previous episode to the class so they also remembered how far she had got. Four weeks later the novel was finished and Angeline began on her next story. This time she invented new characters.

Some stories may be short. Length is not important. One word can be a story, as can a whole page. Both are equally valuable. (See Chapter 3.)

When the one-page rule is broken

Several years ago I worked with a group of teachers who had been developing their approach to Storytelling and Story Acting. One of them came to me with a problem. She had been scribing for a while, but she was beginning to find that the stories her class told her were getting more and more complex. They contained many characters and went on for such a long time that Story Acting was becoming a nightmare.

She invited me into her classroom and asked if I'd lead the acting out of one of them. She handed me a typed sheet of A4 paper. I have written my thoughts on typing verses hand-writing in Chapter 8, but for now, all I will share is that the page she gave me was covered from top to bottom with one story. The font size was an average 12 points, the spacing was normal, the quantity of words was enormous.

As I read through the story I realised it was actually three stories. The child who was dictating had come to a natural end and then started again with fresh characters. As the teacher was typing, she didn't have the natural break of an A5 piece of paper to indicate the end of the page. She had kept typing, and the boy had kept talking.

I tried to lead the acting out, clearing the stage at the end of each section, but even with my experience it was hugely complicated, and I could sense the children getting frustrated.

When I spoke to the teacher afterwards I admitted my difficulty, but I also told her that I would never end up scribing a story as long as that. It was then I realised the strength of the A5-page rule.

As children tell regular stories, they get used to fitting their words onto the page. They become more concise about the characters and the events that are happening, and they develop an awareness of bringing their story to an end.

Witnessing how hard it was to work with a longer story gave me the chance to reflect on the strengths of one aspect of this approach that I sometimes take for granted.

Writing size

My writing is fairly large, and I tend to leave a line between each sentence. This gives me space to make notes after the children have finished dictating. I might record how many baddies there are in the story or how many tigers. Also it gives room for any edits the child might make, either when I read it back or as it is going along.

The size of writing does have an impact on the length of the stories. As the child becomes more confident or if a story looks like it needs more space, my writing gets smaller so that I can fit more in.

Beginning to scribe

The job of the scribe is to record accurately the words of the child.

When they begin to dictate, write their story word for word, exactly as it is said. Allow them to say the whole sentence before you begin scribing. This will ensure you are not restricting the pace of the story. As you grow more experienced, you will discover the optimum speed, guaranteeing that you capture everything they say.

As you write each word, also speak it out loud. This takes practice but is a valuable part of the approach.

Breaking down the process

CHILD: Once upon a time there was a ballerina dancing in her dance class.

As you write the word 'Once' say it out loud, likewise with the word 'upon'. Slow your writing down so that you say and write each word at the same time.

ADULT: Once . . . Upon . . . A . . . Time . . . There. . . Was . . . A . . . Ballerina . . . Dancing . . . In . . . Her . . . Dance . . . Class . . .

Children quickly get used to this process of saying a sentence and then having it scribed. Speaking your dictation means that the child and the scribe are able to set a pace for recording the story that works for them both.

Be careful that the child doesn't slow down for you and end up saying one word at time, as in the example below.

CHILD: There
ADULT: There
CHILD: Was
ADULT: Was
CHILD: A
ADULT: A

It is impossible for any of us to get into a flow when we dictate our stories one word at a time. If this happens, stop writing and invite the child to tell you the whole sentence. Then listen quietly until the child has spoken enough words for you to record.

Talking too fast

Sometimes a child will talk quickly and say long sentences. I always do my best to catch each phrase by saying the full thing out loud. This helps me to remember it.

The more stories you take, the clearer it will become how many words you can accurately keep hold of. Don't be afraid to interrupt the child if you need to so that you can recall what has been said. I am good at memorising long sentences for a short period of time, but beginners may need to repeat the words sooner.

CHILD: One morning the sun came out and then when I woke up I saw a little snail on my hand.
ADULT: (repeating the sentence out loud) One morning the sun came out and then when I woke up I saw a little snail on my hand.
　　　　Okay, let me write that down.
　　　　One . . . morning . . . the. . . sun . . . came . . . out . . . and . . . then . . . when . . . I . . . woke. . . up . . . I . . . saw . . . a . . . little . . . snail . . . on . . . my . . . hand . . .
CHILD: It was a pink snail. And then there was a glittery pink snail.

Figure 2.1 Picture of boy pointing to the word as I scribe

ADULT: (Again repeating the sentence) It was a pink snail. And then there was a glittery pink snail.
    (And then speaking and writing each word) It . . . was . . . a . . . pink . . . snail . . . And . . . then . . . there . . . was . . . a . . . glittery . . . pink . . . snail . . .
CHILD: And then they played with the mummy and daddy and they had seven babies.
ADULT: (Finish scribing the story, still writing and speaking one word at a time)

Another benefit of saying each word as you write it is that this helps children to connect with the process of writing. They often look at their words forming on the page. As a result of their interest, I have seen very young children identifying the word for the character they wish to play.

'I want to be Batman', said three-year-old Kyle, pointing to my book. As I looked at the confidence with which he prodded the word 'Batman', it was clear he'd recognised that those letters and that shape formed the character he wanted to be.

After scribing

When the child has finished the story, read it back to her, underlining all the characters as you go. Take a moment to list these, asking which one the child would like to play.

Draw a circle around that character. Although this story is going to be acted out immediately, it is good to get into the habit of underling and circling characters so that when you take Private Stories, you remember who the child wants to be.

Acting out immediately

Stories taken around the stage are always acted out immediately. This is a vital last step. In this way everyone present knows that his or her stories will be brought to life, in exactly the same way as the stories from the other settings.

Some children may not want to act in their story. I make a note of this at the top of their page. It's not a problem. Sometimes we just want to watch our stories.

After the storytellers have made their choices, the rest of the characters are cast using the other children in the room. This is done in the same way as described in Chapters 1 and 3, by moving around the stage, involving each child in turn, and using verbs to encourage actions.

At the end of the story, clap thank you to the author and the cast.

Private Stories

Once you have demonstrated the process of Storytelling and Story Acting to the group, ask if anyone would like to tell a 'Private Story'. This is described as 'where we sit together, maybe on the carpet, maybe at a table, and I write down your stories, just as I have been doing and we come back later to act them out'.

Make a list of children who want to tell their stories. The group can then leave the stage and head to whatever activity or free play opportunity is next.

A story list

I keep a register of all the children I work with. In this way I can tick their name under the date that they told their story. This record ensures that everyone has the opportunity to get involved. It also means I can keep track of the children who are not coming forward. I continually ask these children if they want to have a go, and I keep a note of their response. If they don't want to, I write the abbreviation DWT (Didn't Want To) in the column next to their name.

The register allows me to share with a child when he last told a story. This list reassures the child that everyone is taking a turn, and it lets him know when it will be his go again.

I visited one class where the teacher had worked out a rota, and every day two children told their stories. One of the advantages of this was that each child knew at the beginning of the morning when it was his or her day to dictate.

Another setting had an elaborate Velcro system, where children's names got moved to the bottom of a silk ribbon once they had taken their turn. The group knew they needed to wait till their names reached the top of the ribbon before it was once again their go.

Whatever your method, it is worth keeping a list of who tells the stories in your group and how often each child gets the chance to dictate.

A child who volunteers and then doesn't speak

Sometimes when a child gets up to tell his story, he freezes. There might be several reasons for this, but it can be hard to know what to do when you sense the child's embarrassment and you don't want to pressurise him.

I used to deal with this situation by letting the child know he could tell his story later.

Then I heard Vivian Gussin Paley speaking on a video, made at a conference in Boston in 2012, where she said, 'There is no later. The job of the teacher is to make it now'. She explained how to make this possible.

> My first and most successful approach to this . . . is to say Jessica has a story, but she can't quite remember it, now if I played with Jessica I would make some suggestions as to what character she likes to play, but you children play with her, and that's how you learn what's on your friend's minds. Jessica, would you like me to ask three people for an idea for a character you might like to tell a story about? Well Jessica, or whoever it is says yes, and the first child is a boy, who says Darth Vader. Unsurprisingly Jessica says no. The point is, eventually one of her friends chooses a topic. You see it didn't matter to Jessica, she's got her topic, she'll tell her story, this is just her first story, but what mattered is that everyone wanted to help her. That's all that mattered . . .
>
> (*Boston Listens: The Wisdom of Vivian Paley*, 2012)

Having tried this approach on two occasions, I have been amazed at how easily it works. For one child, as soon as her friend suggested a princess, she nodded her head. She had found her topic and was eager to begin.

The second time I tried it was with a boy who looked anxiously at the floor the moment he stood up. After I said this sentence, one of his friends helped him to tell a story about Batman by joining him on the stage. Between the two of them they co-constructed a tale. This reminded me of what happens each day, when children play. Sometimes we need friends to help us.

The reason I have tried this only a couple of times is that it is rare that a child steps up to tell a story and then says nothing. Now when it happens, I ask others to help. This feels so much kinder than sending a child back to his place embarrassed.

Reincorporation

When I scribe for several children across the stage, I am fascinated by the connections contained in their stories. Children unashamedly borrow images from each other, adding their own distinct flavour to make each story unique.

Sometimes practitioner are concerned about this, worried that their class are copying each other. But reincorporation is at the heart of creativity.

> Creativity is just connecting things. When you ask creative people how they did something, they feel a little guilty because they didn't really do it, they just saw something. It seemed obvious to them after a while. That's because they were able to connect experiences they've had and synthesize new things. And the reason they were able to do that was that they've had more experiences or they have thought more about their experiences than other people.
>
> (Steve Jobs, as cited by Wolf 1996)

The more experiences you have, the more things you are able to connect, the more chance creativity has to develop.

If we want our children to diversify their stories, we need to feed them a diverse narrative diet, offering them an eclectic range of fictional experiences with which to connect.

In his book Impro (1989), Keith Johnstone makes the link between improvisation, storytelling and reincorporation.

> The improviser has to be like a man walking backwards. He sees where he has been, but he pays no attention to the future. His story can take him anywhere, but he must still 'balance' it, and give it shape by remembering incidents that have been shelved, and reincorporating them. Very often an audience will applaud when earlier material is brought back into the story. They couldn't tell why they applaud, but the reincorporation does give them pleasure.
>
> (Johnstone 1989)

I notice reincorporation in children's stories on a regular basis. It convinces me that we are born with an instinctive understanding of narrative structure. (See Chapter 5.)

Borrowed images

Here are five stories collected around the stage from a kindergarten in Boston, Massachusetts. They are presented in the order they were dictated, and all of them reincorporate characters and ideas from the ones that have gone before, as well as introducing new material. The children are three to four years old.

Liam, age 3

'Two pumpkins, three ghosts; then the pumpkin flew around in a circle, and then the ghost went round in a circle'. (Liam begins the process by telling a short story about pumpkins and ghosts.)

Kori, age 4

'Once there was a butterfly. Then the butterfly flew around in a circle. And then there was a bumble bee. And then the butterfly hiding behind the tree. It crawled and crawled and fell down'. (Kori is next. His story introduces different characters, but he borrows the idea of flying around in the circle from Liam.)

Samantha, age 4

'There was a ghost. And it was hiding behind a tree because there was a monster, and then it made a trap with a net. And it got caught. Then it got cold and it got a blanket'. (Samantha returns to Liam's idea of a ghost, but her ghost hides behind a tree, an image borrowed from Kori's story.)

Marina, age 3

'A butterfly was caught in a net and then a ghost came and ghost found a pumpkin and a pumpkin found a ladybug with a blanket'. (Marina goes next; her story reincorporates the butterfly from Kori's story and the ghost and the pumpkin from Liam's story, but then uses the idea of the net and the blanket from Samantha's story.)

Lily, age 4

'Once there was a princess who made a trap because there was a monster. And then the monster came over to the trap and then the princess opened the trap and then the monster got inside and then a prince came'. (As the creator of the last story to be dictated, Lily introduces new characters, a princess and a prince. She also connects her story to the ones that have gone before, reincorporating the image of the monster caught in a trap that was first suggested in Samantha's story.)

Without conscious effort or working around a theme, the children are inspired by one another. This construction of a class narrative is something I have seen many times during Storytelling and Story Acting.

Building a shared narrative

The following three stories were also gathered around the stage. Without discussion, the children developed a narrative, as if they were trying to find the ending to the first child's story.

Aryan, age 3

'Once upon a time there was a little mouse, and then the mummy mouse went in to cook'. (Aryan begins the process by opening with a story about a little mouse and its mummy. We know the little mouse is outside, because the mummy mouse goes inside to cook.)

Douglas, age 4

'Once upon a time there was a little mouse and she wanted to have a home, but she couldn't. And then the mummy mouse said, "Darling, Come inside, cos it's going to rain". And she squealed. And she said to her mummy, "Mummy, it's stopped raining now, so can I go out and play with my friends?" And she went outside to play with her friends'. (Douglas takes the mouse story further. By introducing rain he gives a reason for the mouse to go inside, well, at least till the rain stops.)

Julia, age 3

'Once upon a time there was a little princess and she need to have a home, but she didn't. And the mummy princess said, "Come darling, cos it's starting to rain". And the little princess went to have tea, and she said to her mummy, "It's stopped raining". And she went outside to play on her slide'. (Julia changes the main character to a princess, but she keeps the idea of the protagonist needing to have a home and a mummy announcing the rain. The princess, like the mouse in the second story, ends up going outside to play, but in Julia's version she has a slide, whereas the second mouse has her friends.)

Each child told his or her story and acted it out, one after the other. The similarities are apparent, but likewise so are the differences. In creativity we take ideas from numerous sources, shaping them to fit our needs and crafting our own individual take on what has gone before.

Three- and four-year-olds understand the fundamental principal of storytelling, it's about making connections among ideas, objects or characters and reincorporating these back into the whole. When children make up stories they act like Johnstone's man walking backwards (1989); they see what has gone before and are unafraid of using the imagery that appeals to them, weaving these into their own narrative.

Introducing storytelling around the stage – summary of points

- Take two or three stories around the stage.
- Be aware of the trust children place in you when they tell you their stories.
- Keep the length of the story to no more than the bottom of the page.
- Although A5 is the best size, remember that stories can be written in beautiful books or on scraps of paper.
- If you choose to type up stories at the end of each session, don't let it get in the way of your enthusiasm to deliver the approach.
- Duplicate or triplicate books offer a way of sharing stories with parents and keeping a copy for yourself.
- Children can add more to their story another day, like a chapter in a book.
- Repeat every word as you write it down.
- Capture long sentences by saying them out loud.
- Encourage children to say more than one word at a time.
- Read the story back to the child and underline all the characters.
- Find out which character the child wishes to play and draw a circle around it.
- Act out the stories immediately.
- Ask if any of the children would like to tell a Private Story.
- Keep a list of who is telling stories and a note of children who don't want to tell a story.
- If a child volunteers and then forgets what she wanted to say, try asking her friends if they know what character might be in the story and see if this helps the storyteller to find her topic.
- Remember that creativity is about reincorporating images.
- Enjoy these connections.
- Feed your class on a diverse range of story experiences.

3   Creating a community of storytellers
Private Stories

There was a princess. Then she went home.
Then she went out again. Then the king come. And the king said
'What are you doing princess?'
'Chasing butterflies!'

(Mira, age 4)

Suddenly everyone wants to dictate a story

Soon after Storytelling and Story Acting is introduced, it becomes apparent that the majority of children want to get involved and will queue for long periods of time, waiting to tell a story.

As mentioned in the previous chapter, keeping a register of who has told a story ensures all children are given this opportunity. You can also let everybody on the list for that day know when their turn will happen. Then they can get on with other activities whilst they wait.

Some children will want to listen to the stories of their peers regardless of whether they are due to dictate. I often have groups of children clustered around me whilst I scribe, taking note of one another's images and deciding on the ones they will they add to or ignore. Storytelling is a communal activity.

Supposing someone never tells a story

There are very few fixed rules for Storytelling and Story Acting. However, there is one that I believe is sacrosanct:

No child should be forced or coerced or feel obliged to tell a story.

This seems very straightforward, but I have seen adults turning to a child and saying,

> Melisa, surely you have a story today. You must have a story; you are such a great storyteller. Maybe you could tell a story about the trip we took to the shops the other day, or you could tell a story about what you like doing. There must be a story in there somewhere; you're not normally so quiet. Perhaps it could be a story about a lion, or a dinosaur, or a monster. Come on, are you sure you have nothing to say?

This is accompanied by the child staring at the teacher or looking down or continuing with what she was doing. Never to my knowledge has it resulted in a story. I wonder in these circumstances whether if everyone stopped talking, that would give the child a chance to speak. But by the time silence arrives, the damage has been done.

Compare this monologue to what happened the first time I saw Vivian Gussin Paley working with a group of children in Indianapolis.

VIVIAN: (Speaking to a boy who has been hovering around the Story Table for a long time)
   Would you like to tell a story?
(The boy shook his head.)
VIVIAN: That's okay; you can be a story listener.
(The boy smiled and seemed to grow a bit taller.)

The next day, the boy was first in the queue to tell a story.

Why do we feel the need to coerce children into doing things? Perhaps we believe it is for their own good; perhaps we expect them to cope; maybe we think that everyone should have a turn. We know how it feels when we are pushed into doing something we don't want to do. Anxiety is the same emotion, regardless of age.

My experience has taught me that if I wait and don't put any pressure on the children, they will always come forward eventually.

Never stop asking or making opportunities available

Although my philosophy is never to force anyone to join in, I believe it is equally important to never stop inviting them to get involved.

On the flip side of coercion there is another issue that feels more damaging.

It is far too easy to write someone off. I have heard it happen in more classrooms than I can bear to count. Someone decides that this group of children can and this group of children can't.

Unfortunately, in my own schooling I was too often placed in the group of children who couldn't. Although that was hard, it does mean I notice and look out for these children now.

I hope you won't recognise any of these statements: *She is too difficult. He's not clever enough. She never joins in. He can't sit still. She's uncreative. He's too shy. She's too loud. It's not worth asking them.*

I've been given all these reasons for why a child might not join in. My thoughts are always the same: he's a child, he might change, or she might see the value of something in a little while that she hasn't seen just now.

Never stop asking.

Every time I do a Storytelling and Story Acting session, I always ask the child who said 'no' the previous week if he or she would like to tell a story. Whatever the child replies is okay. She can be a story listener, and the following week I'll ask her again.

We must give children the opportunity to surprise us.

By regularly checking in this way, I have had many occasions where children with selective mutism have told me their stories.

In one setting there was a four-year-old girl who had never spoken to an adult other than her parents.

Each week I asked if she would like to tell a story, and each week I reassured her that her head-shaking refusal was acceptable.

Then one day she whispered the word "Princess" in my ear. When we acted out the story, she walked around the stage, her head held high, the image of a princess who chose not to talk.

Where to scribe Private Stories

In Vivian Gussin Paley's book *The Boy Who Would Be a Helicopter* (1990), she describes the place where story dictation is taken.

> A large round table we call the Story Table . . . here sit the story tellers, picture makers and paper cutters, watching, listening and sounding forth . . .
>
> (Paley 1990)

Should you decide to create a Story Table, this needs to be an inviting place, filled with activities, like drawing, sticking or bricks. Children may choose to sit and listen to the stories being dictated, cutting and gluing whilst they wait their turn.

Story Tables should be filled with a range of creative materials. Try to be nonprescriptive; otherwise the objects provided might influence the stories the children tell. A table covered in dinosaurs or toy cars will probably results in stories themed around these objects.

One school decided to place a silk cloth on their Story Table to signify to the children that they were taking stories. Another created a Story Hat that the teacher wore whenever she was available to act as a scribe. She walked through the setting wearing the hat, and children with a story found her.

I often end up perched on the floor between a range of activities and a large group of children. Once there I am stuck, until the last of the group has finished dictating. On sunny days, scribing stories outside is lovely, and stories told under umbrellas in the rain can be equally fun.

Figure 3.1 Surrounded by children

The best position for scribing

When you are scribing Private Stories, sit so that the child can see your writing. If all the child is looking at is your elbow or the upside-down book, the opportunity to make the link between the spoken and the written word is lost.

I am right-handed, so I sit the child on my left side. People I know who are left-handed angle their book slightly so that their words can be seen. However you write, take time to think about the view of the page you are presenting to the child.

With the rise in e-mails and texting, how often do children see writing? Don't lose this possibility.

Storytelling is a communal activity

> Our kind of storytelling is a social phenomenon, intended to flow through all other activities and provide the widest opportunity for a communal response.
>
> (Paley 1990)

When a group of children are listening to another child telling a story, sometimes they make comments. At first this can be disconcerting. I have been asked if I want them to be quiet or whether the teacher should move them away. But storytelling is closest to fantasy play, and anyone can join in and suggest ways to shape it.

If a child speaks during the dictation of another's story, it's a form of engagement. It might be they are making a comment: 'I'm going to have a lion in my story'. Other times it's to ask if the lion is going to eat the mouse. This is what happens in children's play; ideas and thoughts come into the arena and act as fuel for the rest of the group.

If someone is intervening a lot, perhaps by suggesting that a certain character, a giant for example, should be included in a friend's story, rather than trying to ignore the child, I turn to the storyteller and ask, 'Do you want to have a giant in your story?'

If the child says yes, then the child has accepted the offer and it will get incorporated into the tale. If not, then I tell the first child that maybe he can have a giant in his own story.

The storyteller has the absolute right to accept or reject the suggestions offered by his or her peers. If another child is persistent, invite the child to tell his own story later. The great thing about stories is that we all have our different versions.

Learning to listen, word by word

The hardest thing about scribing a story is learning to record the words accurately. As adults, we might listen carefully, but sometimes we hear things in the way we understand them, which might not be in the way the child has said them. With very young children, we may get the gist of what they are saying or understand a couple of key nouns, but the difference between scribing a story and having a conversation is that when we scribe we need to comprehend word for word, exactly what is being said.

It is also easy to interrupt or try to steer a child without realising we are doing it. (See Chapter 9.) Perhaps we are asking them questions to pin them down. If a child mentions a star, we may think that it is in the child's best interest to be prompted to describe the star. I worry that such prompting can make the child think he is wrong, and suddenly his star, so clearly seen in his own eyes, begins to lose its value.

There is a time and a place for prompting and asking questions, but Helicopter Stories doesn't need this. Our role is to listen and write what the child dictates and to ask questions only to clarify the points we do not understand.

Despite this, do not be afraid to interrupt a child whose sentences go on for ages. If you want to capture verbatim what the child is saying, you will need to work together to slow down her speech. (See Chapter 2.)

Children do stop talking as soon as you begin repeating their words, and between the two of you, you can set a pace to which you can write.

Some people worry that by interrupting a child they break the flow of their thinking, but whenever I watch colleagues scribing, I am always amazed at how children recall their sentences word for word, even when they have been cut off midflow.

Remind the child that you can't write as fast as she can speak and ask her to help you so that you can record everything exactly as she says it.

A conversation or a story

Sometimes a child will start a conversation before beginning to tell her story. I always try to have an awareness of the difference between when children are talking to me and when they are dictating. This is something that took me a long time to realise, as when I first started scribing I thought I had to write down every word.

Try to distinguish the difference in tone and expression as the child seamlessly jumps from story to conversation and back.

Going from a conversation into a story might look something like this:

ELISA: My story is similar to David's story. It's a scary story, and you only hear it on Halloween.
There were two ghosts and they came out of a well.

The first two sentences are conversation. The storyteller is setting the scene. I don't need to write these words down, although I might refer to them when I introduce Elisa's story to the class.

ADULT: Before Elisa told me her story she said that it was a bit like David's story from last week. She also told me that it was a scary story, that you normally only hear at Halloween. Elisa is going to be one of the ghosts in her story.
There were two ghosts . . .

Conversations sometimes creep into the middle of a story. A child might be dictating about a cat and then stop to ask if you have cat or to share with you that he really likes cats.

ANTHONY: *Once there was a big black cat.*
I've got a cat, I really like cats. Do you have a cat?
The big black cat saw a mouse.

I enjoy watching the seamless way children jump from narration to conversation and back again, with a fluidity that demonstrates how natural story is for them, a comfy slipper that they pull on and slip off as the need takes them.

Silence during Private Stories

Sometimes during a private storytelling session, a child comes forward to tell a story and then falls silent. In Chapter 2, I suggest a strategy for when this happens around the stage, but sometimes in Private Stories it is just you and the child, and you're unable to ask for suggestions from others in the room.

The first thing I do is to give the child permission to think. Quite often the child will put herself into a thinking position and I tend to mirror this, as if I am with her, contemplating. I do this instinctively. I realised only recently how closely my body language gets to that of the child when I am scribing their stories.

Mirroring creates a silent rapport between you and the child. There is research into the feeling of security and closeness that is created when someone mirrors our actions, and I often find myself able to empathise when I copy a physical position. It also informs me whether the person is relaxed or anxious.

I also make sure the child does not feel rushed. After a few minutes I might look at him and smile. After a little more time I might ask if he still has a story or if he wants to play.

Sometimes when I ask this, the child will skip off relieved, and I realise all he needed was the chance to sit and feel what it was like to get ready to tell a story. If the child answers no, we sit for a while longer. I might ask if he knows what character is in his story, or I might wait. Often for these children, all that is needed is time before the story emerges.

When a child is thinking, I ask minimal questions and do a lot of silent listening, rather than filling in the gaps with my own voice. If I had to tell a story, I'd think for a while to take a moment to find my topic and the way I wanted to start. Children are no different. It's hard to reflect when you are bombarded with questions.

A five-year-old boy called Jonathan tried to tell me a story for weeks, but every time he sat down he grew silent. After thinking for a while, he always went off to play.

In Story Acting he was confident, and in conversation he was articulate, but something about the process of thinking of a story got in his way. Too many ideas came into his head. I could feel his brain having ideas and rejecting them and having other ideas and rejecting these. At the age of five, this boy was censoring his creative brain.

Then one day he sat by me and told a satirical tale. It was as if he needed to comment on the situation before he was free to tell other stories.

> One day, when Trish was doing Helicopter Stories, Jonathan really wanted to do one, but he couldn't think. And then his teacher said that his story didn't have to be fantastic. So Jonathan thought of a story that was just a little bit good.

After that Jonathan's stories soared. (See top of Chapter 7.)

One-word stories

Storytelling and Story Acting help me re-examine my definition of story. Children's stories might not contain the standard beginning, middle and end, they may not have a linear narrative that is supposedly essential, and they may be just one word.

In her book *Mollie Is Three: Growing Up in School* (1988), Vivian Gussin Paley encourages the children to share with her their ideas about story. If she is unsure about something, she talks to the children and asks for their opinion.

One incident arose when a boy called Fredrick told her a story. Fredrick hadn't told a story before, although he often listened to the older children as they dictated theirs. As he sat next to Vivian Gussin Paley, ready for his turn, he said one word:

'Fredrick'.

Vivian tried to find out if there was more to his story. She asked questions: what did Fredrick do? Did he go to school? The real Fredrick wasn't interested. He had finished his story, and his story was Fredrick.

When they went upstairs to act out, Fredrick ran to the centre of the stage and smiled. The other children smiled back, but Vivian found herself compelled to

> . . . yield to the teacher's role. *"Is there anything different about Fredrick's story?"* I ask. *"Because he is Fredrick,"* Libby answers. *"Right, but I wondered about a story that has only one word."* John, nearly five, responds quickly. *"It's not one word. It's one person."* Of course. A person is a story. Fredrick need not do something to justify his presence in the story.
>
> (Paley 1986)

One-person stories are fairly common with the younger children I work with.

A three-year-old once told me the story 'Jaws'. The storyteller had never shown an interest before, and even during this dictation, he hovered long enough for me to write his name at the top of the page and underneath it the one word that was to be his masterpiece. Then he was off.

When we acted out his story, he stood at the edge of the taped-out stage, and as I read his one word, 'Jaws', he put his hand upon his head to represent a fin and ran as fast as he could to the other side. As he ran, he hummed repeatedly the first two beats of the *Jaws* theme tune. The other children laughed, and his teacher was enthralled. This was a boy who 'never joined in'.

The unexpected

Adewale was three years old when he came to England. He started at the nursery immediately. I was running Storytelling and Story Acting sessions throughout the first few weeks of his stay. At the time, he spoke very little English. During the first session he willing participated in the acting of stories and seemed quietly confident. After that, when children dictated, he listened, but he always shook his head when I asked if he wanted a go.

Then one day, a few weeks into my time in his classroom, he walked over to me.

'Do you want to tell a story, Adewale?' I asked.

He nodded. Then he looked at me, placed one hand on his chest, and said,

'Adewale!'

I stared at him for a moment.

'Do you want me to write that down?' I asked.

He nodded and bent forward to watch me as I wrote the first line of his story. He smiled, straightened his back and again placed his hands on his chest.

'Adewale!'

'Do you want me to write that as well?' I said, and for the second time that morning he nodded, bent forward and watched as I wrote. A third time he placed his hand on his chest.

'Adewale!'

This time I did not need to ask if he wanted me to write it down. He bent forward and watched my pen move along the paper, writing his name for the third time. And then again, a fourth time and a fifth, exactly the same routine, the same bent head, checking to make sure I recorded his words.

Finally he stood up, raised his arms in the air, elbows bent, hands open, pointing up to the sky:

'And this is Adewale'.

Having finished, he went to play while I pondered on his words.

Adewale, Adewale, Adewale, Adewale, Adewale, and *this is Adewale.*

In the Story Acting, Adewale walked to the centre of the stage. As I read his story, he placed his hand on his chest and repeated the gestures he had used earlier that morning, ending with his arms raised in a celebration of his name.

The other children looked in awe. This was powerful. It touched every one of us. Here was a child, new to the country, the nursery and the language, and he stood before us, proudly telling his story. He had arrived.

Sometimes the pressure of teaching grammar or creative writing means we feel trapped into correcting the words children use or insisting on beginnings, middles and ends. When children dictate Helicopter Stories, they know that whatever they say, it will be written down exactly. Without this, Adewale's story would never have been possible.

Imagine, if filled with good intentions, I had said to Adewale, 'That's not a story, that's your name'. The magic of Adewale's arrival ceremony would have been lost. It is so easy to destroy these moments, to not really listen to what the child is saying or to be governed by our own worries of where a story is going.

By the fourth and fifth 'Adewale' I was secretly concerned. Supposing I filled my page with his name? How could I make good theatre with that? But for me, the lesson from Vivian Gussin Paley is to take those risks, trust where a child is going, even if it seems unclear. By letting the child lead, I hope we will both find answers and take our first steps together at the beginning of their journey.

I have a mantra: 'Trust the child. Trust the child'. I use it when I am unsure. I chant it silently to myself and give the child a moment longer before I judge the situation with my adult brain.

A new once upon a time

> The mummy cook. The daddy watches the telly. And I went on the bus and had dinner with mermaids.
>
> (Jemima, age 3)

Jemima always started her stories with the words *'The mummy cook. The daddy watches the telly'.* After this version of 'once upon a time' she had adventures or travelled on buses to fantastic places, but before any of this could happen she had to establish her norm.

I was with Jemima's setting for ten weeks, so I had plenty of time to scribe her stories. They never deviated from this opening line. The other children noticed it. When I sat Jemima in front of me and began reading her story, the class chanted, 'The mummy cook. The daddy watches the telly'. It became the refrain for all her stories. If this phrase disappeared, we'd have been disappointed. I cringed at the way she saw the world and smiled at how she identified the distribution of labour. But there was something about her intuitive understanding of story structure that touched me.

The quest story-form model always presents the hero in his or her ordinary world. This has to be established before we enter the world of the extraordinary. Jemima's opening phrase, her 'once upon a time', established her ordinary world, before the adventure. Whether conscious or unconscious, there was something grounding about the two worlds contained in her stories.

Prompts for storytelling

I try not to prompt children, but sometimes I find this question can be helpful if used sparingly:

'And then what happens?'

As a reserve question, for a child who is struggling, this phrase may offer a guiding hand. Be careful not to ask it too much, as you may find yourself falling into the trap of asking it after every sentence and then cutting the child off when he comes to the end of the page. This question invites an action which, if overused, can result in shaping the child's story.

When I first started scribing, I didn't understand that young children's stories might contain only characters and little description. In those days I often found myself asking, 'And then what happened' to prompt action.

One day a boy told me the story 'Apple'. Rather than leave it there, I pressed him for more.

'Butterfly' was his reply.

'And then what happened?' I asked, hoping to find the relationship between the apple and the butterfly.

'Cat', he said, followed by 'Duck'.

He looked into the air, and I encouraged him for more. 'Egg', he said. I glanced up to see what had caught his focus. It was then I spotted the alphabet frieze. 'Fish, Goat, House' was his next phrase.

'Is that the end?' I said, desperate not to write down all 26 words that loomed above me.

'Insect', he replied, smiling.

This story is a slightly exaggerated version of what actually took place, but this incident made me question how often I should ask the question 'and then what happened?' Nowadays I prefer to ask 'Is there any more to your story?' This is less judgemental. It sends a message to the child that her story is in her control. One word, or one short sentence, can be a story. As children's narrative language develops, they always incorporate more.

Once the story is over

When the child has finished dictating her story, go through the following process:

- Read the story back to the child, underlining every character.
- Find out which character the storyteller wants to play and draw a circle around it.
- Ask any clarifying questions.

Choices of character

Because children choose which character they play in their own stories, you can find out a lot about what interests them.

Sometimes a shy child will act as the superhero and astonish the room with a confident portrayal of magical powers. It shouldn't surprise us, after all, Superman is a geeky news reporter, and Spiderman is the quiet Peter Parker. When children are taking on heroic roles, it is traditional to wear them as a costume and feel powerful in the land of make-believe.

Sometimes I am amazed for other reasons. A boy once asked to be the flower in his story. There were dogs and children, but he chose the flower. When he acted it out I understood why. As the flower grew, the boy danced around the stage, opening his arms to represent the petals.

I was training Mary Watkins, one of MakeBelieve Arts workshop's leaders, in Helicopter Stories several years ago, when a boy told her a story about a spaceman who flew down to Earth in a rocket. Mary turned to the boy and said,

'I can guess which character you want to play. You want to be the spaceman?'

The boy shook his head.

'I want to be the rocket', he said. She circled it, but when he skipped off she told me that she thought the spaceman was the better character and that she was shocked that he hadn't chosen that one.

When the time came to act out the story, the boy placed his arms in a circle, bent at the middle and span around the stage, making spaceship noises. Mary smiled. Now she understood why he wanted that role.

Afterwards we talked about the danger of assumptions or of seeing the story through our eyes and closing ourselves off to the children's ideas. The boy's spaceship was far more imaginative than either of us could have visualised, but this would have been missed if Helicopter Stories became too directive.

Mary still acknowledges this event as 'one of my biggest learning experiences. Trust the child and you get moments of magic'.

Clarifying questions

Once a story is finished, you may need to ask questions to clarify the actions. It might be that you want to know if the 'he' that is mentioned later in the story is the Prince from earlier. It might be that you are unsure if the storyteller wants some children to play the house or the castle. Ask questions that will help you to lead the acting out.

Number of characters

If there are any characters, where the number is unspecific, ask the storyteller the quantity she requires once the story is finished. For example, there may be baddies or fairies in the story, and you have no idea how many there should be. If the child says a high number, say 100, use this time to negotiate, being realistic about how many children will fit onto the stage and how many there are in the group.

Be careful you don't limit the number of some characters and not of others.

Supposing ten fairies seem manageable, so you readily agree to have that number. Then another child asks for eight baddies and this feels too large.

The vital last step

Once you have taken several Private Stories, you are ready to go back to the stage and act these out, completing the process with the vital last step.

Scribing Private Stories – summary of points

- Keep a record of children who want to tell a story and those who already have.
- Never coerce a child into dictating a story.
- Let children who don't want to tell a story feel positive in their role as 'Story Listener'.
- Keep asking children even if they don't say yes immediately.
- Remember that storytelling is a communal activity.
- If you create a Story Table, fill it with a range of creative materials.
- Always refer back to the storyteller to check whether he wishes to include characters suggested by his friends.
- Understand that the hardest thing about scribing is hearing exactly what young children say.
- Try to distinguish between when a child is having a conversation with you and when she is dictating her story.
- If a child decides not to speak during Private Story dictation, wait and don't pressurise him.
- Understand that children's one-word stories actually contain *one character*.
- Try asking 'Is there any more to your story?' if a child stops talking for a while.
- Once the story is finished, ask any clarifying questions that will enable you to support the acting out.
- If there are several of one character, check how many there are supposed to be once the story is finished.

4 The vital last step
Story Acting

Once there was a princess. And she was trapped in a tower.
And the good fairy come, and the bad fairy come, and together they melt the tower.

(Leila, age 4)

Leila's class have been doing Helicopter Stories for nearly two years. She attends a school in Lewisham that is one of MakeBelieve Arts' Helicopter Centres of Excellence. There are a number of these centres across the country, and they consist of settings where staff have been trained in the approach and are committed to incorporating Helicopter Stories into their classroom on a weekly basis. For an up-to-date list visit www.makebelievearts.co.uk/centres-of-excellence/.

When Leila finished her story, she told me she wanted to be the princess during the acting out. The time arrived, and Leila stepped onto the stage. I invited three children to join her. They stretched up their arms, just as she instructed, creating a tower. In her role as the princess, Leila stood inside, holding onto the walls and gazing over the heads of the children seated around the stage and out into the distance. The princess was trapped.

When we reached the part of the story where 'the good fairy come' and 'the bad fairy come', two new children entered the stage and worked together to bring this image to life. Raising their wands, they cast their spell. They needed no instructions on how to do this. It's an unwritten part of the story, an archetypal image which they intuitively understood; fairies, regardless of whether they are good or bad, wave wands to create magic.

Slowly the children forming the tower began to melt, falling to the ground, beat by beat, dissolving. Princess Leila looked around her, and, seeing that the tower had disappeared, she stepped over the linked arms and walked to freedom.

The story ended; the audience clapped.

Although the story is short, when we see Leila and the other children act it out, we uncover the full extent of the narrative. Leila knows exactly what her tower looks like and is able to arrange the children around her to form this structure, extending their arms upwards to form turrets.

Entering the tower, Leila immediately goes into role, holding onto the arms of the children and peering outside the walls of her prison. The children playing the tower are aware of the importance of their role and stand completely still. The scene is absorbing for the audience, and yet we are sat on the floor of a dusty classroom and the actors have barely started school. We are transported to another world, a world where princesses are locked in towers. Our imagination, like Leila's, has filled in the gaps, and through her eyes we see our own version of the surrounding landscape.

For the children involved in the deep play-acting of this story, the effect is powerful. The good and bad fairies also fill out the story, reflecting each other's movements as they simultaneously wave imaginary wands. It takes a lot of concentration to mirror another person in a live performance, but in Story Acting children as young as three do this instinctively.

When the tower is melting, the three children creating it show further expertise. They fall, deciding without words that they will do this gradually, enjoying the moment of collapsing to the floor.

The involvement of the actors develops the story. Their interpretation brings the narrative to life, creating pictures in the mind of the audience.

This is what happens in theatre, and it is the same regardless of whether the actors are in a classroom or on a professional stage.

Leila's story ends with the tower breaking, but maybe one day the full novel will emerge, and we'll find out the reason why the good and bad fairy joined together to free the princess.

A vital last step

By guaranteeing that all the stories are acted out on the day they are taken, we ensure that Storytelling and Story Acting is a living activity that breathes life into the words of the children. This is the vital last step. It allows us to dig deeper into a narrative and is a valuable approach for storytellers, regardless of age.

Jane Katch (2002), author and fifth-grade teacher in the United States, uses Story Acting to support older children in developing their creative writing. She finds it helps a child to reflect and to think about what works and what doesn't. Having watched her class, I was impressed with the clarity this gave to the authors and the enthusiasm in which they approached further editing. (See chapter 10.)

> Stories are not private affairs, the individual imagination plays host to all the stimulation in the environment and causes ripples of ideas to encircle the listeners.
>
> (Paley 1990)

The storyteller

The character that the storyteller is playing was circled during story dictation. Before you start the acting out, take a moment to remind yourself of this. That way you won't forget to include them. Believe me, in the fast-paced world of Story Acting, I have seen it happen.

The expert in your midst

The storyteller is the inventor of the narrative and holds all the knowledge about the story. If another child is hesitant, ask the storyteller. She knows how each character moves or how she wants the children to stand to create the house. If an actor struggles, invite the storyteller to demonstrate. If you need clarity on any point in the story, question the storyteller. If the story says the children are playing a game and you don't know what game they are playing, ask the storyteller.

You have an expert in the room. How fantastic to use them.

If for some reason the storyteller doesn't have the answer or is reluctant to share it, ask the other children:

'I wonder what game the frogs might be playing in Alisha's story'.

When someone responds to this question, repeat their thoughts back to the storyteller. 'Amanda thought the frogs might be hopping. Is that was they were doing?'

The offer is then either accepted, or the storyteller suggests another activity, or other children try to work out what the frogs might be doing.

This kind of questioning becomes interesting for everyone in the room. It demonstrates our care for the words of another child and our desire to get his vision right. What were the frogs playing? Will we ever work it out?

For those of you whose narrative brains have kicked in and who will be disappointed if you don't find out what the frogs were doing, I have it on good authority that they were flying around the garden on roller skates.

By checking with the storyteller we empower the author with ownership, but we are also reassuring the actors that anything they are uncertain about can be answered by the story's creator.

When the storyteller is also a director

Sometimes a storyteller takes responsibility for directing his story, as Leila did at the top of this chapter, moulding the other children into the shape of the tower. You will notice the children who have an eye for this, as they will automatically tell everyone on the stage how the characters in their story moves or the objects stand. When a child has very set ideas about staging, it can be hard to let him explore these in depth.

Maybe there is a worry that the child is taking over or that he is leading too much, when in our work we are trying to allow all the children to find their own solutions. Before rushing to rescue the actors, spend time observing and, where necessary, supporting the social interaction their negotiations open up. (See Chapter 7 for examples.)

Alongside its numerous benefits, Storytelling and Story Acting gives an opportunity to find out more about the children in our settings, the ways they relate to each other and the support they need to communicate their ideas.

Choosing

The storyteller should not choose which roles other children take in her story. Although it is important she have control over all other aspects of her work, casting is the one area where she does not get to pick. When a child asks if she can have her friend acting in her story, I tell her that when I do Helicopter Stories I believe it is fairer to invite children to be involved from around the stage; that way everyone gets a turn.

If children choose who takes part in their story, Story Acting will become an activity that some children may never have a chance to participate in.

Take a moment to reflect on your experiences of choosing at school. For some of you it may be positive; maybe you were the child who was popular and good at sports and everyone wanted you.

Or maybe some of you were more like me.

When it came to sports, I was the second least likely person to be selected. The first least likely person was Julie. When Julie was in school, it was a much better day for me, as I always knew there was one person left unchosen after me and I wouldn't be the very last child to join the team. Unfortunately for me, Julie was hardly ever at school, so most days, I was the girl who was pointed at when everyone else had been chosen. I hated it. I am sure Julie hated it more.

When given the power to choose, children often involve their friends in their stories and those that do not fit into these friendship groups become excluded.

It is unfair to put this pressure on a child. It is hard for any of us to select someone to work with who is not our friend. Supposing we do approach someone new and our friend gets upset; or what if the person we want to work with doesn't want to work with us? At least with our mates we know we are safe.

I have heard teachers deal with the issues that arise out of selection by inviting children to choose someone who has not been chosen yet by saying, 'Austen hasn't been in anyone's story for ages; why don't you let him be the lion?'

Often such questions are followed by the phrase 'I don't want Austin to be in my story'. Imagine how Austin feels.

Another way of dealing with this was confessed to me by a teacher I was working with. She used to say to her class, 'Put your hand up if you haven't been chosen'. We joked that what she was really saying was 'Has anyone got no friends? Put your hands up if no one wants to work with you'.

Going around the stage and taking turns in the order of where children are sitting stops any of this exclusion, and those who are introduced to the approach in this way quickly grow accustomed to it. By taking it in turns, they get the chance to experience different methods of being together. Friendship groups blur as children act with peers they would not normally play with.

A teacher from Boston who moved to this way of working from a selection model told me how beneficial her children were finding it. Her class had begun to work well together, outside Storytelling and Story Acting, which she said was an unexpected advantage. One of the boys who didn't make friends easily but who excelled in acting out had started being invited to tea with the other children. He had been accepted into the classroom. 'It was as if the group had noticed he was there, and I'm sure this was a result of seeing how well he acted as a monster in a couple of the other children's stories'.

The blades spin

A teacher who has delivered Helicopter Stories for a number of years once asked if the reason we called it by that name came from the way we select children to be involved in the action, by going around the stage, taking it in turns. She compared this to the blades of a helicopter spinning around. I love this idea, and it is a great way to remember this process, but the name actually comes from the title of the first Vivian Gussin Paley book I read, *The Boy Who Would Be a Helicopter* (1990).

Blurring gender roles

Another benefit of taking children from around the stage is that you never know what part they will play in someone else's story. Gender roles become blurred. A group of girls might end up as the baddies, or a boy may become a princess; the shy child can be the superhero, the lively child the walls of a castle, and these roles may differ to ones they take in play.

What's my motivation?

I was working with a group of children who were experienced Storytellers and Story Actors. Michael told me his story. It was about a character called Ben 10, whom I knew, and another character called Vilgax, whom I hadn't come across. Assuming the children all knew who this was, I didn't ask Michael any clarifying questions before we started the acting out.

One of the benefits of taking children from around the stage is that you never know who will act out each character. That was the case on this day.

Michael wanted to play Ben 10, and it was Jane's turn to be Vilgax. She did this willingly, but when I asked if I could see her walking like Vilgax, she whispered to me.

'What's my job? What do I do?'

I asked for help.

'Michael, how should Jane move when she's acting Vilgax? Have you any ideas that would help her?'

Michael looked at me and replied, 'Vilgax is very tall, bigger than Ben 10 and he's grey'.

I fed this back to Jane, hoping to give her something to play with. She continued to stare at me and then asked, 'Yes but what is my job? How do I know how to move if I don't know what I'm supposed to be doing?'

It was a great question, and because it was whispered to me I repeated it to the storyteller.

'Michael, Jane wants to know what Vilgax does – is he a baddie or a goodie?'

'A baddie', said Michael.

I relayed this information to Jane and asked if she now had enough to work with. She smiled at me, walked onto the stage and looked suitably mean. She had found her motivation.

She reminded me of the professional actors I work with at MakeBelieve Arts. They often ask for more information before feeling confident to try out a role. They might need clarity on the back story or the characteristics of a person they are playing.

Both these children were five years old and had been doing Storytelling and Story Acting since nursery. I guess I shouldn't be surprised at how professional they were.

Negotiation

Although the storyteller is in charge of his story, sometimes another child will come onto the stage and ask to be a character that is not included in the narrative.

'I want to be a Thunderbird'.

If this happens, one way to deal with it is to ask the storyteller. 'Is there a Thunderbird in your story?'

If the storyteller says no, try asking a question. 'Billy says there isn't a Thunderbird in his story; I wonder what we should do?'

Often during this kind of negotiation I stop speaking for a while and allow the children to find a solution. If I do speak, it is to check with one child or another, whether the offer that has been made reaches their approval. Children are used to negotiating in this way. They do it regularly in play.

If there is no compromise, I explain to the child who wants to be a Thunderbird that in this story there isn't one and that maybe, when he tell his next story, he could include a Thunderbird in that. (See Chapter 7 for more examples of negotiation.)

> Commentary is welcome at any time, but permission is required to insert a new character into someone's story . . . Do your actions belong in the scene you enter? If not, can you convince the players to alter their script or, failing to do that, will you agree to a different role? We call it socialization, which simply means-at any age-that you agree to play your part acceptably well in the given script.
>
> (Paley 1990)

Helicopter Stories is one step up from play, which is a flexible tool that children are used to discussing and controlling. Helping children to facilitate these conversations is valuable, but I try not to find the solution for them.

The Pirates Code

In 2003 film Pirates of the Caribbean, Joshamee Gibbs says to Elizabeth Swann that the Pirates Code is more like guidelines, insinuating that they should forget about the code and forget about the rules; after all, they are pirates. Whenever I reach that moment in the film, it always reminds me of how I feel about Helicopter Stories.

There are very few hard and fast rules to Story Acting. Every time I suggest anything, you may discover that in certain circumstances another possibility works better. Consider this book to be one of guidelines, which should be instantly ditched if the alternative is more suitable.

As long as children are at the centre of this activity and the reflection is ongoing, Story-telling and Story Acting will have a powerful impact on a group. At a conference in London in 2003, Vivian Gussin Paley said, 'If something isn't working, we need to change the way we run the activity, not the way the children approach it'.

The importance of choice

When working with a group to act out their stories, I prefer to have all of them present. Sometimes a teacher will ask if she should take a particular child out of the room, because she is 'on the autistic spectrum' or because she is 'hard to engage'. I always discourage this. Helicopter Stories are for all children, and regular use helps to develop communities. It would be doing the group a disservice to exclude certain members because they do not conform to specific norms.

One boy I worked with, who was autistic, wanted to stay in a wigwam near the stage whilst the acting out took place. As the first story happened, he poked out his head. During the second story, his whole body came out; by the third story he had crawled behind one of the other children and was peering around them. After three weeks he eagerly sat next to the stage as soon as the tape was laid down.

We must return to the Pirates Code. The suggestion that all children should be present for Story Acting is guidance. It depends on the needs of the individual. I have seen adults pin children down in a cuddle to make them stay for a carpet activity. But breaking the spirit of a crying child also breaks the heart of a group. Some children need to walk around. If a child leaves the circle and wanders the classroom, as long as there is someone who can watch him, as long as the child is safe, then where is the danger? The appeal of this activity is such that most children want to stay.

Taking part

Taking part in the acting out is also a choice. If certain children don't want to, it is not a problem. Keep asking, every time you reach them in the circle, and always accept their response. It is rare that a child will refuse for long, and normally within a few sessions every-one is happy to get involved.

Sometimes a child will not want to act in her own story. This is fine. It can be thought-provoking to watch your story unfold without your involvement. If this is what the child decides, sit her in front of you so she can see the action, consult her on any movements or moments of confusion, and clap thank you to her and the actors at the end of the story.

Bola spoke very little English. Initially reluctant to tell a story, when his first one, 'Tiger,' emerged, he was adamant he didn't want to act it out. Sitting in front of me, he watched another boy from his class crawl around the stage, growling and eyeing up the audience as if stalking his prey. Bola's face shone with enjoyment. Choosing not to perform was as valid an experience for him as if he had chosen the leading role.

Watching our stories brought to life validates our voice. We realise we are worth listening to and that the group enjoys acting in our tales. We may even notice something that we hadn't seen before. It did not take long for Bola to begin Storytelling and Story Acting on a regular basis, but this first step was vital in his journey to being heard.

No one should enter the stage unless he or she is involved in the Story Acting

Although this guideline is there to delineate the stage, there are times when this can be ignored. The Pirates Code comes in handy.

I have worked with several children who find it impossible not to step onto the stage when it is not their turn or when others are engaged in acting out. Sometimes it's hard to be tolerant of this, but there are individuals in every classroom who need extra freedom and are not yet ready to sit still.

If a practitioner continually tries to get one child off the stage and that child becomes tearful or angry, it will break the trust of the whole group. Also, as soon as our focus is diverted, it is highly likely that the child will wriggle back.

In a DVD featuring Vivian Gussin Paley, titled 'The Boy Who Could Tell Stories' (2001), Aaron walks uninvited onto the stage during the Story Acting. Here is a transcript of this moment.

VIVIAN GUSSIN PALEY: The puppy walked all around the tree.
(Two girls stand on the stage. One is playing a puppy and one is playing a tree. Aaron rolls on the floor grabbing at them and giggling.)
VIVIAN GUSSIN PALEY: Aaron, you stand up and be a tree too. Let's find out if Aaron would like to be a tree in our story.
(Aaron continues to roll around the stage.)
GIRL: Aaron's kind of different in our class.
VIVIAN GUSSIN PALEY: Aaron's kind of different in this class? Aaron, can you be a different kind of tree?
GIRL: He don't know what you are talking about because he don't know . . .
VIVIAN GUSSIN PALEY: No, I think Aaron could be a flower or a tree.
AARON: A tree.
VIVIAN GUSSIN PALEY: Stand up and be a tree then, two trees, let's change our story.
(For a moment Aaron stands still, and then he wanders outside the stage area, watching.)

The majority of children understand the need to remain seated and don't react when the child who has more difficulty with this instruction is given extra freedom. We all know when someone's 'kinda different'. We want them to have support.

If allowing one child this freedom developed into a problem where all the children climbed onto the stage, then I would have a conversation about it and let the group find the answer. However, working in this way with different classes for more than 15 years, I have never found this to be the case. Children are naturally empathetic.

Equal or fair?

Is treating everyone equally always fair?

Helicopter Stories is a step up from play and has a similar chaotic sense of rule and order attached to it. Children's needs are as individual as each child in the room. Some children need more one to one time than others; some children struggle with the process of socialisation, of finding their place in the group. Story Telling and Story Acting is a vehicle for supporting this, helping children to explore different roles and to see each other in a different light. When children need extra support, I continue to remind them of the rules and allow them the space to engage.

Examining fair

'I want my friend to be the mum in my story', announced a three-year-old during Helicopter Stories.

I reminded her that when we do stories we use children from where they sit around the stage. Her friend had just had a turn, and we were working our way around the circle. It was currently another child's go.

Benita thought about this. 'So what about her?' she said, pointing to girl who sat on the other side of the stage. 'It's not fair that she has to wait. When is her turn?'

I reminded Benita that the girl she was pointing to had also had a turn and was one of the mouse's friends a few stories ago. I reiterated that she was waiting for us to go all the way around the stage again so that she could have her second turn.

Benita thought some more. 'What about him?' She pointed to another child a little bit closer to where I was sitting.

'He was up just now', I said. 'He was the tiger'.

'And him?' she asked.

'The walls of the house', I said.

She indicated a few more children, all of whom had already taken a turn on the stage, and at each point I reminded her of the character they had played.

'We keep going around the stage so that everyone gets a turn', I said. 'I just want to make sure it's fair'.

'It is fair', she said, and happily allowed the child whose turn it was to be the mummy in her story.

Having been allowed to question the rules, she was content to carry on, safe in the knowledge that the thing she valued most, fairness, was being upheld.

Logistics for Story Acting

Timings

I normally allow at least 20 to 30 minutes for Story Acting. This gives enough time to act out between five and eight stories. However, some settings take Helicopter Stories every day and regularly act out two or three stories at the end of each morning. This can take as little as five minutes.

If you are new to leading Story Acting it is probably worth starting with a few stories per session and gradually building this number as you become more familiar with the approach.

Some stories are short or straightforward to act, and others are more complex, so it's worth keeping an eye on the length you are getting in the early days and using these as a gauge to how many you can scribe in one session. This will ensure you don't run out of time for the acting out.

All stories must be acted on the day they are taken, even if you are rushing for the bus at the end of the afternoon.

Storytelling and Story Acting is a live experience, and it is vital that we don't forget the Story Acting part of it. This is the vital last step. It is the part that engages children and connects this work to play. Now their stories have a purpose, and this provides motivation, particularly for children who don't normally get involved in literacy-based activities.

Settings often gather Private Stories throughout the session and then act them out as the final activity. Story Acting is fast-paced, and it needn't take long.

A regular basis

For this approach to work it is vital that it takes place on a regular basis. In Vivian Gussin Paley's classroom, Storytelling and Story Acting was a daily occurrence. In many settings in England it takes place once a week, and in other places around the world it is a mixture of daily and weekly. To get the full benefits of this work, it must happen frequently.

If you take an average class of 30 children and scribe six Helicopter Stories once a week, it takes five weeks to get through every child. If the same class were to tell three stories a day, each day of the week, every child would have turn in just two weeks.

The more regularly the children experience dictating their stories, acting them out, and engaging in the stories of the other in their classrooms, the more impact the approach will have.

Props

The reality of Helicopter Stories is that props are not necessary. Children can use their bodies to become buildings or objects, or they can mime them. They do this in fantasy play.

Imagination makes it possible to see a whole world inside your mind, and acting in this world enables you to bring an audience with you, painting the picture for them. We do not need to clutter the stage with props and make this process cumbersome. It would necessitate a vast array of objects to keep pace with the requirements of the stories and would add nothing to the value of the work.

The speed and the immediacy of Helicopter Stories is a huge part of its appeal and benefit. Story Acting is improvisation. It is an opportunity for children to imagine and for the practitioner to discover how the group sees the world and how this is portrayed to the audience.

The smallest of movements often tell the largest stories.

Story Acting – summary of points

- Story Acting has the power to transport us to another world.
- The involvement of the actors brings new aspects of the story to life.
- For older children, acting out stories can be used as an editing process.
- The storytellers choose which character they wish to play in their story.
- The storytellers do not choose which children are in their story.
- Roles are allocated by going around the stage in turn.
- When we work in this way, gender roles are blurred.
- Consult the storyteller if there is confusion on how a character moves or an object stands.
- If the storyteller is unsure, ask the other children.
- Allow the storytellers to direct the action (if they choose).
- Support children to negotiate with each other, exploring solutions together.
- If something isn't working, change the way you run the activity, not the children.
- Remember the Pirates Code; it really is just guidelines.
- Treating everyone equally is not always fair.
- Allow 20–30 minutes for weekly Story Acting session and 5–10 minutes if you are acting stories every day.
- Make Helicopter Stories a regular classroom activity.
- Ensure all children are present.
- No child should be forced to act in a story.
- Some children won't want to act in their own story.
- The approach doesn't need props. These can be imagined or created using the children's bodies.
- Story Acting is a fast-paced activity.

Helicopter Stories: The four stages of introduction

A summary of the how?

http://youtu.be/UkJl8dyzRQQ – a ten-minute video of Trisha Lee running a Helicopter Stories

Equipment

- Masking tape
- Two or three introductory stories
- An A5 book or A5 sheets of paper for scribing stories
- A pen
- A register

Stage one: Introducing Story Acting

- Mark out a rectangular stage and invite the children to sit around it.
- Read an introductory story, stopping after the first sentence to enable children to begin acting out the roles.
- Move around the stage, selecting children in order of how they are seated, one after the other.
- At the end of each story ask the children to clap thank you to the actors.

Stage two: Scribing a story around the stage

- Ask if anyone would like to tell his or her own story.
- Invite the first child to sit next to you.
- Write the child's name and the date at the top of the page.
- The story can be as short as the child likes, but it can't be any longer than the bottom of the page.
- Write the story verbatim, repeating the words out loud as you scribe.
- Read the story back to the child, underling all the characters as you go.
- Draw a circle around the character the child wishes to play.
- Immediately the story is scribed, lead the group in acting it out.
- Once you have scribed and acted two or three stories, ask if anyone would like to tell you a Private Story.

Stage three: Private Stories

- Private Stories can be scribed around a table or with the teacher and the child seated together, side by side on the floor.
- Sit so the child can see what you are writing.
- Storytelling is a communal activity. Other children might sit and listen.
- The storytellers can decide to include or reject the ideas of their peers.
- Write exactly what is said and say each word out loud as you scribe.
- Stories can be one word.
- No child should be forced to tell a story.

- Read the story back, underling the characters.
- Ask whom the storyteller would like to play and draw a circle around this character.
- Ask any clarifying questions that help you understand but do not change the story.
- Tick the child's name on the register.

Stage four: Story Acting

- All stories should be acted on the day they are taken.
- Sit the storyteller in front of you, and tell the group which character he or she is playing.
- Read the first sentence; then move around the stage and invite children to take on the other roles
- The storyteller is the holder of the knowledge about the story.
- No child should be forced to act.
- Once the story is finished, clap thank you and move onto the next story.
- Keep a list of who would like their story scribed for the next session.

Approach this work with curiosity and play . . .

Section II

The why

Storytelling and Story Acting

Who are these people who dare to reinvent mythology? They are the children found in every classroom thinking up plot and dialogue without instruction. And for the most part without the teacher's awareness.

(Vivian Gussin Paley 1990)

5   The enchanted place

Why is story so important?

> Going on a bear hunt.
> He went to go to the cave.
> And then a bear come and say 'raa'.
> And then he tried to eat them.
> And then they ran home, through the snow storm, and they went home.
> They locked the door, and the bear wanted to be friends with them.
>
> (Martha, age 3)

Three-year-old Martha was so engaged with Michael Rosen's story 'Going on a Bear Hunt' that she readily followed in the tradition of oral storytelling throughout the centuries and narrated her own version. She recalled many of the stories details – the cave, the snow storm, the locking of the door. She also changed the ending. In Martha's version the bear wanted to be friends, which is logical; even a three-year-old knows that life is so much easier when we're able to befriend the bear.

This act of hearing a story and then reshaping and retelling our own version of it takes place amongst children in every country across the world from an early age. It happens regardless of their background, their living conditions, or the amount of food in their bellies. Children in wartorn countries are as eager to engage in make-believe tales as those from middle-class suburbia.

And stories are not just the playground of children. As adults we spend vast amounts of time consuming, creating and sharing them. From the first cave dwellers, who made up legends to explain the world around them, to the people of the twenty-first century who sit watching films or reading books, story has always had a powerful role in our lives. When we sleep, our brain uses story to process the events in our unconscious mind. Story is the method we communicate with, huddled around the water cooler or in the staff room, sharing with friends our tales from the weekend. We often creatively colour these, like all good narratives, to add dramatic flavour, reinventing our lives with a sprinkle of exaggeration and a sparkle of magic.

When adults tell stories

At the first training session I ever delivered I asked a volunteer to dictate so that I could demonstrate scribing. I still have this first adult story, and I remember the way it was acted out.

> One day there was a mother who went home, opened the front room and found that the dinner was cooked, the house was quiet and that the children were playing nicely.

When I asked the teacher which role she wanted to play, she smiled and said, 'The mother, of course'. We acted it out. One of the teachers became the door that the mum opened as she entered the house. We created a stove made out of two teachers, and a third played the dinner bubbling away. Finally, when we came to the 'children playing nicely', I asked how many there were. She told me 'four'.

The teachers who took on these roles sat smiling angelically at the mother. The stove and the dinner bubbled away in the background, and the mum surveyed the scene with a look of joy and relief. As we clapped thank you and cleared the stage, I noticed that the author sighed. I asked if she really had four children. It was no surprise that she did. My next question was whether she ever came home to such tranquillity. She shook her head.

How wonderful to use Storytelling and Story Acting as a way of experiencing our dreams, creating the perfect homecoming, after a day at work, escaping for a moment the reality of our lives.

At a conference, in front of 1,500 people, a man told a very different story.

> Once there was a tote bag at a conference. It had thousands of tote bag friends. But no one came to get them. So it sat there, disappointed, waiting for someone to come. They didn't. Eventually the tote bags were given to passers-by.

It turned out he was one of the organisers. I will leave you to guess what area he was in charge of. But it's not only adults who use story to mask their anxiety. This is exactly what children do when they confront the monster or hide from the dragon.

A fundamentally human thing to do

Listening to and telling stories has always been a fundamentally human thing to do. If this function served no purpose other than to help us pass our time on this earth, then surely, over the centuries, it would have become redundant.

So why do we engage with stories, and what benefit do stories serve in the lives of the children we work with? In his book *Consciousness Explained* (1991), Daniel Dennett explores the way evolution has produced creatures that are able to maintain the 'distinction between everything on the inside of a closed boundary and everything in the external world'. This can be seen in tribal or pack behaviour, the home and its defined borders protecting us from the dangers of the world outside. It is equally as relevant to beings that survive on their own, like the snail, growing its shell to create the boundary between itself and everything external to it.

There is security in the known, and survival depends on our being clear where safety ends and danger begins. Dennett compares this evolutionary process to the occurrences that takes place in humans as we develop our sense of self. He believes that narrative gives us a method to govern what goes on both inside and outside our personal boundaries, providing us with the ability to self-protect, self-control, and self-define.

> Just as beavers build dams and spiders spin webs, people tell stories.
>
> (Dennett 1991)

Dennett proposes that it was out of our evolutionary need for preservation that we began to spin tales. He calls this the 'centre of narrative gravity', which instinctively unifies all the fragments of information it comes across, as if they were from a single source. In the stories that we share, we unconsciously construct the image of ourselves that we project to others, and we also make sense of the world and how it is portrayed to us. The fact that this is done, for the most part, without our conscious awareness results in our having an instinctive understanding of narrative structure and metaphor. This is present as much in young children as it is in adults.

But where do they come from?

Our tales are spun, but for the most part we don't spin them; they spin us.

(Dennett 1991)

This notion of the unconscious nature of story resonates with the work that I do in theatre and improvisation. Often during the devising process, ideas seemingly come from nowhere, as if everyone in the room has tapped into the same supply line but no one quite knows where it was or how we found it.

Long-form narrative improvisation consists of groups of actors creating hours of interconnected stories in front of an audience with no prior rehearsal or discussion; they are just making it up as they go along. Watch any group of children engaged in deep play where they are telling a story or becoming characters, and you will see an improvisation troupe, also making it up as they go along.

Narrative runs deep inside us, and when we open ourselves up to it, we never quite know what stories will emerge. Then, some days, those creaky, uninspired, grey days, nothing comes.

Elizabeth Gilbert, author of *Eat, Pray, Love*, spoke about this 'elusive creative genius' in her TED talk (2009). Searching for answers as to why the imaginative source is sometimes there and at other times you feel as if you were wading through treacle, she finds herself revisiting the belief system of ancient Greece and ancient Rome. She discovers that in those days, 'people believed that creativity was this divine attendant spirit that came to human beings from some distant and unknowable source, for distant and unknowable reasons' – a web that we spin, that we're not in control of.

Story proof

In the book *Story Proof* by Kendal Haven (2007), this senior research scientist turned professional storyteller sets out to uncover the science behind the astonishing power of story. He examines how our brains are evolutionarily hardwired to think in story terms and presents evidence to show how we seek out narrative connections within the information we are given.

Here is an example of one of the proofs that can be found in his book.

Here are three sentences.
He went to the store.
Fred died.
Sharon went hungry and cried . . .
Did you assume that the 'he' in sentence one is Fred? Did you try to connect the first two sentences and wonder if Fred died because he went to the store, or while at the store? Did you presume that Fred went to the store to get something for Sharon to eat? Did you assume that Fred and Sharon were connected and that she wept in part because Fred died?

(Haven 2007)

Even though the sentences above are disconnected, our minds unconsciously create a story that joins them.

Haven demonstrates how easy it is for us to relate to something once it is presented as a story. He believes that narrative works as a natural and flexible teaching and learning tool, a superhighway to the brain.

> Story is emerging as the interstate express carpool lane into the mind. Why? Just as traffic engineers designed those specific lanes to speed traffic into major cities, so, too, evolution and the brain's experience during its plastic years have engineered story pathways as express routes into the human mind.
>
> (Haven 2007)

A rehearsal of reality

But what is the point of this fast lane, and what does it enable us to do?

Jonathan Gottschall, author of *The Storytelling Animal* (2012), shares how psychologist Keith Oatley describes stories as 'the flight simulators of human social life . . . stories safely train us for the big challenges of the social world. Like a flight simulator, fiction projects us into intense simulation of problems that run parallel to those we face in reality'.

Story offers our brains a flight simulation of the events contained within the narrative, so we go through the ups and downs, but thankfully we are still alive at the end. We haven't suffered the unattainable love or faced the danger of certain death; our heroes have done this for us, and we have wept alongside them.

Oatley proposes that although we enjoy engaging with stories, nature developed our ability to do this, to enable us to practice situations, encountering them in our minds, rather than waiting till we meet them in real life.

The more I think over this concept, the more connections I make between my work in theatre, which in essence is about creating and sharing stories to engage audiences in thinking in other ways, and the participatory approach of Augusto Boal, explored through his Theatre of the Oppressed (1979).

Boal was a Brazilian theatre director who developed an approach called Forum Theatre. The actors create a short play that rotates around a central protagonist and the escalating difficulties the protagonist faces as he tries to achieve his goal. At the end of the show the character is in a worse situation than he was at the beginning. The Joker/facilitator speaks to the audience, asking if they see any places where the action could be changed in a way that would alter the consequences of the story. The play starts again, and the spectators (or Spect-actors, as Boal names them) are empowered to stop the action at any point and take on the role of the principal oppressed, trying out different solutions. This is defined as a rehearsal of reality, a flight simulator that enables us to engage with problematic situations without actually getting hurt.

Glance in the dolls corner of any nursery or reception classroom and you see children readily engaging in their own rehearsal of reality, trying out the role of a mother searching for a lost child, or burning the dinner, or being cross. We see princesses and superheroes, monsters and dragons, confronting danger, challenging evil or running home to safety in a helicopter, where they know the doors can be shut and the bear can be left outside.

Aristotle was the first to notice the paradox in fiction, in that it gives pleasure but most of its content includes events that are unpleasant. A story where there is no adversity, where everyone is happy and nothing happens, is of no interest to anyone. Struggle and hardship are the essential ingredients of narrative. Kieran Egan, in *Teaching as Storytelling* (1986), talks about the importance of binary opposites – for example, good and evil, fair and unfair, cruel and kind – as vital story components, and he believe it is our desire to explore these global concerns that engages us with fiction.

And then the neurons start to fire

When we look at the power of story from a neurological point of view, it gets even more exciting. Science has shown that when we connect with a story, parts of our brain related to a particular emotion or action light up. Our neurons start firing as if we were engaged in the activity ourselves and not just passively reading about it.

In a 2006 study reported in the *New York Times* (Murphy 2012), researchers asked participants to read words that were linked to strong odours whilst their brains were being scanned. What they discovered was that as well as the receptors that deal with the processing of language becoming engaged, other relevant parts of the brain lit up, as if the person were actually smelling lavender or cinnamon. They established that when we hear words with strong connotations, our brains react as if we were actually perceiving them. Researchers also learned that when we read about people engaged in actions, the motor cortex part of our brain becomes active as if we were physically involved too.

We now know that there is an overlap in the part of our brain used when we are trying to figure out the thoughts and feelings of other people and the part that we use when we make sense of stories.

> Narratives offer a unique opportunity to engage this capacity, as we identify with characters' longings and frustrations, guess at their hidden motives and track their encounters with friends and enemies, neighbours and lovers.
>
> (Murphy 2012)

Two studies that were published in 2006 and 2009 by Dr Oatley and Dr Mar concluded that individuals who are exposed to greater quantities of fiction are more able to understand, empathise and see the world from the perspective of others than people who have less exposure.

In other words, stories have the power to affect us physically, and nature makes sure that we enjoy them, because they are good for us.

> Human life is complex, the stakes are high, and fiction allows our brains to react to the kind of challenges most crucial to our survival as a species.
>
> (Gottschall 2012)

And all this begins at a very young age. It is easy to believe that it starts at the onset of language, but the more psychologists learn about newborn babies and their capacity for 'rhythmic, purposeful consciousness', the clearer it becomes that children are making narrative connections long before words are learned.

> . . . even very young infants appear to communicate with an artful imagination, ready to pick up new expressive tricks. They try to move with others to learn how to live in fictional, meaningful, historical ways.
>
> (Trevarthen 2010)

The enchanted place

Children are attuned to stories; they can't wait to hear them and are eager to tell them. When we listen to their dialogue at play, it becomes clear how much of their endless streams of consciousness and metaphor is borrowed from the many sources available to them. These images are placed together in different orders, presenting a picture of the world and how it is seen through their eyes.

Story is a vital tool for children, for it offers a place for them to explore and make sense of the various words, sights, sounds, tastes, smells and textures that bombard their senses each day. By taking on roles in fantasy children experience different situations and empathise with the perspective of others.

A. A. Milne's book *Winnie the Pooh* ends with a reference to the enchanted place that exists within the Hundred Acre Wood, where Christopher Robin and his bear continue to play. One of MakeBelieve Arts Helicopter Deliverers, Annekoos Arlman, shared this as the way she felt when she first started scribing stories using Vivian Gussin Paley's approach (MakeBelieve Arts Helicopter Stories, internal evaluation, 2014).

It was like 'being invited back to that Enchanted Place on top of the Forest, which most people leave, far too early. It is at once very familiar and yet strange, because after all, I no longer live there, I am just a visitor. But while I am there I fall under the spell so easily, it's as if I've never been away'.

Above all, even beyond the evidence of neurological connections that story makes for us, it is something as simple as this sense of entering an enchanted place that drives me to listen to, to scribe, to re-create or make up stories of my own. This is a world that all of us can enter.

The here and now

Peter Brook said that 'theatre exists in the here and now. It is what happens at that precise moment when you perform, that moment at which the world of the actors and the world of the audience meet. A society in miniature, a microcosm brought together every evening within a space. Theatre's role is to give this microcosm a burning and fleeting taste of another world, and thereby interest it, transform it, integrate it' (Nicolescu 1990).

This immediacy, this here and now of the theatre, is also present in the classroom when children come together to act out their stories. The way that theatre ignites its audience can happen whether in a classroom 20 minutes before the end of the morning or in a darkened auditorium at an evening's performance by professional actors. The theatre of the children portrays a microcosm of the world as they see it. Their questions, explorations, fears or sense of adventure are explored through the world of play.

Storytelling and Story Acting allows for these thoughts to be shared, borrowed, worked and reworked by all the children. Gathering together as an audience, as a community, they learn the stories of each individual, borrow ideas and add their own, share with each other approaches to acting, portray characters and develop narrative that are unique to each classroom.

> We rely on stories like we rely on air, water, sleep and food . . . Stories have started feuds that have lasted for generations . . . They have changed societal and cultural attitudes,

beliefs and values, as well as swayed public opinion . . . They have changed and continue to change the world – to define our world. Stories can be amazingly powerful – frighteningly powerful.

(Haven 2007)

And yet so often we take them for granted.

Storytelling is an intrinsically human thing to do.

(Haven 2007)

6 Stories we may not want to hear
Guns, superheroes and taboos

The army tank was in the war and then an army gun.
An army person shot the bad team.
Of course the grey team was bad.
An army speed boat came and he had a gun because it was attached to the army boat.
The army Chinook came and it was shooting down at the bad guys.

(Sam, age 4)

Sam lives in Kent. Like many of the children in his class, his dad is away in the army. To connect with his father Sam makes up stories about wars, army tanks and shooting. His home is filled with images of the army. He knows the word 'Chinook'. Even at five he could draw pictures of this two-headed helicopter-like machine, which I needed to look up in order to understand what he was talking about. Sam's world and his terms of reference are built around the norms of life in the army. This is Sam's story. Each time he tells it, it changes slightly, but it always revolves around a similar theme.

Zero tolerance

I have shared Sam's story a few times with groups of teachers, and some of them were surprised that it was 'allowed' to be acted out. In settings where gun play isn't acceptable, a story like this would have been stopped during the scribing stage.

Whenever zero tolerance of gun or superhero play comes up, I find myself asking the following questions.

Supposing Sam had been told that he wasn't allowed to tell war stories? What if guns had been banned from his classroom? How would a ban on his style of fantasy play have helped him to find his way, a safe way, in the classroom, where he felt secure to act out and make sense of the reality of his life outside school?

I ask these questions, knowing that years ago, when my son was small, I would have hated Sam's story. I might even have gone so far as to ban stories like that if I had been running Helicopter Stories at the time. Now I feel embarrassed at this truth.

In the early 1990s, as the single-parent mother of a boy child, I felt it was my role to protect my son from growing into a violent man. I had lived at Greenham Common Women's Peace Camp in the 1980s and was actively involved in the women's movement. My belief in pacifism meant I spent hours searching for water pistols for my son that weren't shaped like firearms. I hunted charity shops for dinosaur- or dolphin-shaped pistols, all in a bid to avoid buying the Deluxe Super Soaker Pump Action Gun that was my son's heart's desire.

One day, I watched as he cut off the ends off a skipping rope I had given to him and turned it into Indiana Jones's whip. I found myself mentally trying to find a compromise between what I could justify to myself as acceptable male fantasy play behaviour based on action adventure heroes and unacceptable male fantasy play behaviour that was too close to the military I had spent so much of my teenage years and twenties protesting. I started justifying my decisions to myself: Indiana Jones needed a gun because he was an explorer and that could be dangerous, whereas if my son was pretending to be in the army, that would be a different type of aggression. I was trying to find a way to validate the play that my son was enjoying but also to balance this with the political discussions I had taken part in during my early involvement in the peace movement.

Luckily I found Penny Holland's book *We Don't Play with Guns Here* (2003) before my neurosis did too much damage. In this book, Holland looks at the culture of zero tolerance that built up in the 1970s and 1980s and that still exists in many settings in the UK and in the United States today.

First, she set out to find evidence of when the zero-tolerance approach became common place. Interestingly, she was unable to find any trace of a written mandate that banned guns or war toys from early-years settings, although, according to everyone she spoke to, there was a unanimous feeling that zero tolerance was a local authority policy.

Next, she learned from ex-employees from the now disbanded Inner London Education Authority that there was no written policy that they could remember but that there did exist a general feeling at the time that this type of play should not be encouraged. Finally, by interviewing practitioners who worked in early-years setting over the past 26 years, Holland discovered that zero tolerance was often an unwritten rule, which she believed had more to do with individuals' own feelings than with a considered educational policy around this area of play.

> Feminists were engaged in raising a number of hypotheses in relation to the causes and effects of male violence based on empirical evidence. Violence is not experienced theoretically and the need to act in immediate ways to intervene in the spiral, took ascendancy over the need to elicit scientific proof of cause and effect. Perceived sexist patterns in children's play presented themselves as an area in which women could take some control.
>
> (Holland 2003)

Having examined the 1988 Sutton-Smith investigation of studies that explored the link between gun play and subsequent male violence, Holland revealed that there is no evidence that makes it possible to conclude anything certain about this relationship. There are no longitudinal studies in this area, and the short-term studies Holland explores either disprove any increase of aggressive play as a result of exposure to war toys or are flawed in that they fail to distinguish between play fighting and real aggression or the novelty factor of these toys on the children who played with them.

When gun play is banned

In her *Early Education* journal article 'Bang, Bang! Gun Play and Why Children Need It' (2003), Diane Rich sums up some of the reasons she has heard for why settings follow a practice of zero tolerance:

- Guns are wrong. Guns kill. It's wrong to kill people.
- It is morally wrong to promote anything that can harm others.

- Guns mean violence and aggression. If we allow children to play with guns they will become more aggressive.
- Parents don't like it.
- Other children get upset.

The list she gathered was extensive, although she added that whenever she talks to practitioners about this issue, the comments usually end with 'but they do it anyway'.

Having worked in many settings where zero tolerance is still in effect, I have witnessed boys build Lego guns and then pretend, when questioned, that they are hair dryers or mobile phones. It is interesting that the need to outlaw guns in early-childhood play has generated a far more damaging consequence – the condoning of creative lying, particularly from boys.

Another danger, particularly for children like Sam or those children who are allowed to engage in gun or superhero play at home or whose parents are part of a rifle club, is that school becomes a place that is alien to their outside life experiences.

Penny Holland also explores how banishing this type of play affects the girls in a setting. She observes how girls are praised for being involved in the passive activities of drawing or playing in the dolls corner and how boys are more likely to be told off for being physical and running around. The girls, watching the boys getting told off, decide not to try out more physical activities. Some settings don't encourage girls to be physical because their passive play gives the staff fewer problems. By practicing zero tolerance, Holland suggests, we also continue to replicate the stereotype of the female in a less active role.

It amazes me how personal preference has had such a moderating influence on the fantasy play of both boys and girls in early-years setting without any scientific evidence to prove that gun play is damaging.

I know from my own parenting that my beliefs made me question and analyse the toys my son had access to and the programmes he watched. I also faced the conflict between how he fitted with other boys of his own age and my mixed emotions from observing the enjoyment he gained from superhero and gun play stories. Many teachers I have spoken to feel this conflict, and there is often an uneasy relationship between supporting fantasy play that incorporates fighting and squaring this with our own feelings about weapons.

> There is a tendency to look upon the noisy, repetitious fantasies of children as non-educational, but helicopters and kittens and superhero capes and Barbie dolls are story-telling aids and conversational tools. Without them, the range of what we listen to and talk about is arbitrarily circumscribed by the adult point of view.
>
> (Paley 1990)

Stage fighting

Supporting children in acting out stories that contain fighting can be difficult, particularly if we are used to discouraging this in our settings.

How I deal with this is to say to the children that when we have fighting in a story, it is important not to touch each other so that nobody gets hurt. These are the stage directions of fighting. This is how actors fight.

I have seen incredible dance-like fight scenes between children using this rule, where they move in slow motion and avoid knocking each other. I have also seen children continuing this beautiful way of play fighting outside the stage area, practising not touching and enjoying the control and discipline afforded by these movements.

One teacher who was previously anxious about the levels of play fighting in her setting reported to us that after several weeks of regularly delivering Helicopter Stories, she had overheard two children talking. One boy said to the other that if there was fighting in the game they were playing, they mustn't touch. Story Acting allows us to support children in learning the stage rules for how to play without hurting, to kick without touching, and to fall without bruising.

When pretend doesn't work

As I mention in Chapter 1, one of the phrases I use a lot when I am working with a group of children, is the word 'pretend'.

'Pretend you are fighting, without touching'.

When I worked in a school in a township in South Africa, where the children spoke Xhosa as their first language and were just beginning to learn English, I struggled to make them understand what I was saying.

When three lions and three tigers meet and the lions want to eat the tigers, what do you do if the children you are working with do not understand the English for the word 'pretend'?

I watched as three pairs of heads locked together, pushing against each other, whilst the faces beneath growled and roared. Sometimes the lion was the strongest and the tiger moved backwards, sometimes it was the tiger, but no one was hurt. It was play, and the children were safe, although for a while I was anxious.

The same problem arose a second time during the session. 'Pretend the spiders are climbing up a tree. . .' Normally this small word, 'pretend', is enough to get a five-year-old miming, but not these nine-year-olds. 'Pretend' isn't covered in the English-language curriculum, and I didn't know the word for it in Xhosa.

So a boy played a spider, suspended from the shoulders of a second boy who played the tree, and it all happened too fast for me to notice, too fast for me to stop for fear it might hurt, too fast for me to work with the class to set the rules on their play. So by the time I noticed it, it looked beautiful and safe. And I wondered how many other beautiful and safe things I have missed, because I used the word 'pretend' too soon or said 'gentle' in expectation of rough.

I had another experience where the word 'pretend' failed me, in a classroom where I worked on and off for several months. In the Story Acting, Tom was playing a monkey, and the monkey was climbing a fence. Stevie had taken on the role of the fence. I asked Tom to 'pretend' he was climbing, and then I watched as he lifted his first leg of the ground. He was completely engrossed in his role, and before I realised what was going to happen, he also lifted his second leg. So deep was his engagement that there was a moment when even I believed he would stay in the air, but of course gravity prevailed, and he and the fence toppled gracefully to the floor, laughing.

At the time, I remember being surprised at the ease with which the two boys fell, and again this made me question the anxiety I feel to keep things safe and how much skill children have in playing and falling without getting hurt. Of course, sometimes children do get hurt, and of course we want to protect against this, but these moments remind me that I mustn't rescue too soon, particularly in the territory that children are most familiar with, the rough and tumble of play.

Count to 20 and die

The most frequently asked question that Vivian Gussin Paley receives is how to deal with violence in children's stories.

When in September 2012 a group of Boston public school teachers asked her this question, she replied by sharing with them an experience she had had in Baltimore several years previously, in an area where zero tolerance of gun play was prevalent. She was demonstrating her technique with a group of children in front of 150 Baltimore teachers when the following situation took place.

> A tall, rather mature looking kid knew right away that I didn't know about the zero tolerance, so he told me a very quick story, action packed, the good guy killed the bad guy, dead, and I could hear the intake of breath. Bang, Bang, Bang, he added. Well I believe a guest must not do anything to embarrass the host if possible, now who were my hosts? The children, not the other guests, the children . . . So I knew that the boy's story had to be acted out, otherwise that would be an embarrassment. Storytelling is not meant to embarrass people. But to confirm the notion that we will find the way to tell everyone's story.
>
> (Cited in Lee 2011)

Vivian asked which character the boy would like to play. He replied, 'the bad guy'. Vivian let him know that this was fine, adding, 'But listen to the stage directions: the bad guy can die to the count of 10 or the count of 20'.

She then told the boy that with each count, he needed to move further and further down, till he lay on the ground dead. He mustn't stop moving till the final count.

The boy chose to die over a beat of 20.

'And I will tell you, that the Ballet Theatre of New York would not have done a better job'.

The adult audience were amazed at the control and beauty of the boy's movements, as he slowly edged his way to the ground, in an approach that made it feel more like a dance than something they found unacceptable.

Problem solving

One of the reasons for anxiety about children pretending to fight on the stage has to do with safety and ensuring that no one gets hurt. When I feel this way, I try to use the experience as an opportunity to problem solve with the class, to uncover ways we can keep safe and still have fun.

In one setting I worked with, a group of boys had a spell of telling stories about football. These stories often involved one boy kicking to another boy and then to someone else, and the result was a blow-by-blow match play of the passing needed between friends in order to score a goal.

On the day these stories first emerged I went to the Story Acting stage with six versions of this tale from different boys in the class. As I read the first one I realised it was going to be difficult. As Andrew passed to Leyton, the kick of the boy playing Andrew was so high in the air that I became frightened that the other children would get hurt. The story progressed, and by the end of it all the children were delivering the highest kicks they could and I was becoming nervous.

Knowing I had five similar stories in my hand, I told the children about my anxiety. I praised them for the way they had managed to act so sensibly so that no one got harmed, but I also told them I had other football stories and I was unsure what to do, as the kicks felt dangerous on our small stage and we had no room to expand the size of it. I asked the class for suggestions.

One child proposed a rule that they always kick low to the ground. The others agreed, and we practised this move. As we read the second story, a pass happened, and again the child delivering it lifted his leg high in the air, narrowly missing one of his friends. At the end of the story I asked the class for help as the 'keeping our feet low' idea wasn't working.

This time a child suggested that that kicks happen only at one end of the stage. This worked a bit better, but there were too many children involved in each story for it to feel entirely safe. Eventually the group decided that only four children could be in a football story, and each of them had to run to one corner of the stage and kick in the air whenever a pass happened in the match. Amazingly this worked, and for a while the class and I had great fun playing with this bizarre rule, which came entirely from children problem solving how to make the acting feel safe.

When thousands acted in the story of a five-year-old

On November 15, 2013, I was working in New York, when I heard on the news the story of a five-year-old boy who was in remission from cancer. The Make-a-Wish Foundation had put out a call for volunteers to transform San Francisco into Gotham City for a day so that the boy could act out his fantasy of becoming Batman. Thousands of people came forward, and during the day the boy, dressed in a superhero costume, had the opportunity to battle the Joker, rescue a mascot and be presented with the keys to the city.

I remember at the time thinking how incredible it was that a whole town could join together to act in the superhero fantasy play of a five-year-old child. How powerful, that the desire of this boy to be Batman touched the hearts of so many, reaching that deep-seated need in all of us to play, to act out our stories, to immerse ourselves in a world where we can battle monsters and win.

As I listened to the news, I reflected on a conversation I'd had the day before, during which a practitioner had told me that superhero play was banned from his setting. He spoke about how concerned he was as he watched the boys constantly told off when these fantasies materialised. I echoed his concern, and we spoke for a while about the importance for children of confronting their monsters. I also talked about how in Storytelling and Story Acting there is an opportunity to share bad-guy, good-guy play with the whole class, to investigate it and discuss how it makes us feel. And then we talked about how difficult it would be to involve all children in Storytelling and Story Acting if we were to dictate the type of stories they were allowed to tell. One of the greatest benefits of Helicopter Stories is finding out what really matters to each child.

As I watched the news, I thought about the man who was deeply unhappy in a setting that banned superhero play, and I wondered whether his school would have allowed the Gotham City exploits of the boy who fought cancer. Somehow, this boy's Batman fantasy stimulated the imagination of a whole city, and everyone wanted to join in the game.

When 7,000 people turn out voluntarily to take part in a boy's superhero play, then surely this is evidence of an intuitive understanding we have of the value of unrestricted fantasy in our lives.

The Seeing Place

> 'The word theatre comes from the Greeks. It means the seeing place. It is the place people come to see the truth about life and the social situation'.
>
> (Stella Adler)

I came across this quote the other day, and I got very excited. I love the idea of theatre as a Seeing Place. I began to make the connection between this and the Seeing Place that children reveal to us when we give them the opportunity to share their stories in the classroom.

In theatre, whether the theatre of children engaged in fantasy play or the theatre of adults in a rehearsal room, when it works we find ourselves tapping into a powerful force. In children we call this deep play. In adults we call it a good day's work, and we return home with a skip in our heart and a twinkle in our eye that is hard to explain to anyone who wasn't in the room. We know we are onto something.

Theatre is a place where we can dig for the truth, ask the questions that need asking and search for possible answers. When we share our truths with an audience, we invite them into our Seeing Place, giving them the opportunity to see the world through our eyes. When we tape a stage to the floor, we build a Seeing Place in our classrooms, opening a doorway to the world of children, a chance to share in their wisdom.

In 2014 I was privilege to work with a group of five- and six-year-olds in Melbourne. I delivered a Helicopter session in a first grade classroom. A boy, Manish, age 5, told his story across the stage, and while he spoke, the children around the edges laughed and held their breath and were filled with anticipation.

> Once upon a time the lion had a house with lots of food. And then the pig walked through the jungle and he saw the house. And then he ringed on the bell and went into the house. And then the lion let him in. And then he asked if he could get some food. And after he got the food, they became friends.

When Manish got to the part about the pig walking through the jungle, the laughter started. I asked one of the children about the laughter. I wanted to make sure that the boy beside me knew that the giggling was with him, not at him.

A girl looked at me and said, 'A pig, just walking through a jungle, it's going to get eaten'.

As Manish continued and the pig approached the lion's house and rang the bell, the tension in the room was palpable. As one the class anticipated that bloodshed was imminent. As the lion let the pig into his house, one boy closed his eyes and screwed up his face.

'He's going to die', a girl whispered,

Laughing, Mannish completed his story. Not wanting to face this monster, he chose to create friendship, not fighting, between this unlikely pair, and several of the children sighed with relief.

Having had a front-row seat into the Seeing Place of this classroom, I left with my own feelings about what we had shared and a greater understanding of the humour and the investigations on friendship that were taking place. If I had been able to come back another day, maybe I would have learnt more about the world where two different animals that aren't supposed to like each other have the opportunity to be friends.

As I look back on that morning and think about all the fighting that is happening in the world, I find myself asking if there is a message in Manish's story. In a land where lions and pigs can walk into each other's territory and become friends, I find myself wondering about the potential for this vision, shared with me from the Seeing Place of children, to become a reality.

Making sense of the world

Alongside superhero play and tales of animals taking risks, sometimes the stories children share are filled with images and situations that have happened in the world, either at home or on the television. Storytelling can be a powerful way of trying to make sense of these events, and acting them out can serve as a cathartic experience.

Resa Matlock, director of the Ball State University Child Care Collection, told me a story about a child she was working with when she first started incorporating Storytelling and Story Acting into her work.

Anthony dictated his story: 'My baby sister died of SIDS. That's spelled S-I-D-S'.

I still remember, all these years later, that when Resa first told me about this boy, she also told me how unsure she had felt about whether it was right to involve the class in acting out this true story. After seeking advice from a colleague, she decided to go with it and see what happened.

As the class began the Story Acting, the children took on various family roles. Anthony played himself. While the story was acted, he fed in some of the sentences his mother said during the day; another girl played the piano; another sang. One child stepped forward to say a few words. As Resa and her colleague sat at the edge of the stage, they watched these children present a truth that had affected one of their peers, and they were amazed at the empathy demonstrated.

Weeks later, at a school event, Anthony's mother spoke to the team, confirming their belief in the value of the drama they witnessed.

'You don't know how much this has helped', she said. 'He kept wanting to talk about it'.

Acting in stories and fantasy play offers children a way to try to comprehend things that have no logical understanding. When they act these things out or watch others acting out, they have the opportunity to explore a vast range of human emotions. This is no different to what happens in the theatre or in a film, when we connect with the actors and empathise with their story. Because the stories we are acting in the classroom come directly from the children, what better way for us to get an understanding of what is going on for them and for them to use theatre to make sense of their world?

9/11

One day in September 2002, just after the first anniversary of September 11, a child in reception class told me a story. This was a boy I had worked with when he was in the nursery the previous year, and so he knew Helicopter Stories.

> Once upon a time there was a plane, and he was going to crash into a building and make an explosion. And all the people were hurt. And they got to die. And then the firemen came and then the firemen put out the fire'.

The story is chilling. During acting out, the children were totally engaged. I felt unsure, out of my depth. Could we deal with this issue with five-year-olds? But I trusted the child.

He wanted to play the plane. I was worried that it would be trivialising an issue, but I went with my gut feelings and let him set the tone of the acting out.

Before we acted it, I asked how he wanted to show the building. He was very clear and pointed to a place on the stage. That was where the building was. He didn't need it to be represented by a child. We started acting.

The boy plane flew to the spot and then gently curled into a ball on the floor. I brought up five children to play the people. They very seriously took on their roles of being hurt, and when I read 'they got to die' they all lay down on the floor in total silence.

The room was hushed; all the teachers and children were engaged in the action. Then I called up another five children as the firemen. They stood up and walked among the bodies of their classmates, earnestly holding imaginary hoses and putting out the fire. We all watched in stunned silence. It was the closest Helicopter Stories has come to drawing tears from me, and all of us, from the youngest to the oldest in that room, were moved.

When we clapped thank you and cleared the stage, there was a moment of quiet reflection, and then almost as one the children looked at me and said, 'Can we do it again?'

I was surprised; I didn't know what to do, so I simply said, 'I'm curious to know why you are so keen to do that story again'. A girl sat next to me, looked up and said, 'Because it was really interesting'. So we did it again, because where I was confused, the child was right; they knew that we had tapped into something really powerful, something that school and adults don't often let us tap into, a way of exploring our fears and the things that we don't understand and of giving voice to the thoughts that we all have and that often we try to protect our children from discussing.

Expressing fears

It is rare that the previous two types of stories come up, and when they do, each situation needs to be looked at individually. I have never had a Disclosure Stories, although I've been asked lots of questions about whether they do get told. Sometimes I hear metaphors in stories that make me ask the teacher about a child. 'Daddy is a monster' could be a story about a dad who plays monster games with his children or about a dad who is cruel. Knowing the children in your class will give you an idea about such metaphors, but it is important not to look for things that aren't there.

Story is the place where children express their fears. One girl told the same story every session for six weeks. It was about getting lost and her dad finding her. She always played her dad, and the getting lost would happen in various locations – the woods, the supermarket, the street. Eventually the teacher spoke to the parents, and it turned out the girl had wandered off in the supermarket when she was with her father. The story was her way of examining getting lost, a story she needed to play out until she found her resolution with it. She never acted the part of herself; she knew that role. What she wanted to understand was what it was like to be the one who searches. In her acting out she always looked worried and clearly demonstrated the actions of looking without finding. Maybe this was the picture she had created from conversations with her parents.

Another thing that sometimes comes up in children's stories is the occasional mention of poo or wee. Again these are rare, but when they happen I tend to write them down and during the acting out I skim over it. 'The dog did a poo and then walked in the garden'. During the acting out I ask to see the dog walking in the garden, but I never ask to see the dog doing a poo.

Of course, all things from children's lives will come up from time to time if you use this approach regularly. Storytelling and Story Acting gives children a voice for their thoughts, their concerns, their laughter and their questions, but it also offer us, as practitioners, a way to discover the deliberations of a child. Why then would we ever want to censor it?

> I regard the theatre as the greatest of all art forms, the most immediate way in which a human being can share with another the sense of what it is to be a human being.
>
> (Thornton Wilder)

In Storytelling and Story Acting, what greater way is there for children to explore and share with one another their sense of what it is to be human, and what better window can you think of as a Seeing Place into the world of your class?

7   Facing the monsters
Solving problems from a safe space

Once upon a time there was a man. His name was superman.
One day he was flying back to his home when he heard that someone was saying
'Help Me, Help Me'. Then he flied back down to where the
'Help Me' person was, and he was battling a dragon,
because the dragon was hurting the person's feelings.

(Jonathan, age 5)

Story has the ability to connect us with the emotions of a character, whilst at the same time distancing us from the personal aspects of our own circumstances. Knowing that good overcomes evil can help us face things that feel difficult or unfair in our own lives. Metaphor allows us to explore these issues safely. It is far easier to learn how to battle our dragons than to be a five-year-old facing a world that is big and scary.

Jonathan's story shows he understands that there are different ways to hurt. By becoming a superhero who rescues the 'Help Me' person, he takes on the role of supporting a friend. But this is not a fire-breathing dragon; this is the worst kind of dragon, for it hurts people's feelings; it attacks at the core of its victims. To tell this story Jonathan shared his knowledge of this different kind of pain. 'The dragon who hurts people's feelings' is a strong metaphor, a way to explain the burning when you ache inside.

The strength of engaging in this kind of storytelling is that we support children to develop their ability to think in metaphor. If we can use these to solve problems or examine situation from a different perspective, then it becomes a useful tool.

In one classroom Isla Hill saw the potential to incorporate children's knowledge of story as a way of changing one of those sticky moments that sometimes happen in groups, into a chance to find a solution as a group.

Sleeping dogs and cockerels

Jake was three years old. He was fairly new in the setting, and we were informed by his teacher that he was 'struggling to adapt to the rules of nursery'. She confided in us that they were having problems with him and that we needed to be careful as he was inclined to want his own way.

When Isla introduced Helicopter Stories, Jake started to cry. When she asked him why, he said he wanted to tell a story. She patiently stopped scribing for another child, acknowledged how Jake felt and asked if he could wait. His turn would be next.

He nodded, and I noticed his teacher glaring at him. When Isla invited Jake to tell his story, he skipped over to her, smiling widely. It was about a puppy that ran around, barking ferociously at everyone before lying down to sleep. It was interesting to watch this boy puppy, barking at all the other children around the stage, warning them not to come near and yet bouncing around like a young dog, sending a mixture of messages: stay away from me, play with me. As I watched I could sense his struggle, trying to settle in this new place but fighting it at the same time, afraid it might hurt.

When Jake lay down to sleep at the end of the story, we all clapped thank you. But Jake didn't move. Isla invited him to come and sit back at his place and we all clapped thank you, but still Jake didn't move. He lay on the stage, with his eyes closed, pretending to be asleep. I could just make out the grin on his face at the game he was playing. Isla congratulated him on the story and asked if he would come and sit down. Jake was caught in his game, and I could see his teacher looking awkward. She wanted to lift him off the stage, but we had asked to manage the behaviour of the group and I could sense her disproval of how we were doing. We needed to act fast. The preferred method in these situations is to ask the children what we should do. I am always surprised by their answers.

'The puppy Jake is asleep on the stage, and I don't know how to wake him', said Isla.

'Maybe he needs an alarm clock', said Matthew. 'Beep, beep, beep . . .'

'Perhaps we could tickle him awake', said Meena, wiggling her fingers in a tickling motion as she spoke.

'Or we could be a cockerel and wake him up in the morning. Cock-a-doodle-doo, Cock-a-doodle-doo, Cock-a-doodle-doo', said Andrew.

The rest of the class joined in, and the sound of cockerels filled the air. 'Wake up, Jake, Cock-a doodle-doo', said Andrew, leaning into the stage from where he was sitting. And as the cockerels crowed, Jake the puppy began to stir, got onto his four legs, wiggled himself awake and crawled to his place around the stage.

The cockerels, having finished their crowing, joined Isla in clapping thank you, and we smiled at the teacher. She nodded and later said it was not the way she would have dealt with it, but Isla and I were pleased. Jake had returned to his seat with no tears, and Isla had handed the problem to the children, rather than trying to deal with it herself.

Fredrick is a robber

In Vivian Gussin Paley's book *Mollie Is Three* (1988), Vivian demonstrates how she learned to incorporate narrative into her classroom. In this way she was able to support a boy called Fredrick, who had difficulties following some of the classroom rules. He grabbed paintbrushes and Play Doh from other children; he knocked over a ship made from blocks and did a lot of furious yelling.

Taking the lead from three-year-old Libby, who used story form to engage Fredrick as a father rather than a robber (because robbers can't play in the dolls corner), Paley found herself using the same approach one day, asking a frustrated Fredrick whom he was pretending to be. It stopped his tears immediately.

'Do you want to be a bad guy or a good guy?'

(Paley 1988)

Fredrick wanted to be a good guy and sat contentedly watching as the rest of the children continued to play. Later, at the snack table, Christopher asked if Paley was still mad with Fredrick, and when she said 'no', he questioned her further. Mollie stepped in:

'Because now Fredrick is nice'.

'And before?' I ask.

'That's because he was a robber'.

Fredrick, she knows, plays many different roles. She can better explain his behaviour as a character portrayal, than in terms of classroom rules.

(Paley 1988)

In *White Teacher* (Paley 2000), it is a girl named Sylvia who sometimes has problems conforming to the rules of play. One day she takes on the role of 'bad baby' and begins to pull out all the dishes and pots from the dolls corner cabinet and throws them over the floor. Rena tries shouting at her in role as the mother, but Sylvia screams back. Ayana steps in, threatening Sylvia with not playing together if she doesn't pick up the dishes. Sylvia wants to play and begins reluctantly to pick them up. Ruthie saves the day, turning Sylvia's actions into a game:

'Pretend we just move in . . . the moving man dropped all the boxes and now we have to put everything away on the shelf'.

. . . Rena dials the telephone. 'Mr Moving Boss, we won't pay you because it was a bad job'.

Everyone was laughing as she hung up. The equilibrium was re-established.

(Paley 2000)

Recently I received an e-mail from a teacher who had attended a training session I ran. She was excited by the potential of narrative to help children to make sense of their choices and sent me the following paragraph:

One of the little girls, who can get angry very easily, became so excited about listening to the stories, making up her own and acting them out. One of her stories featured Cinderella. Later in the day when she got angry, I said to her, 'What would Cinderella say?' This calmed her down and helped her to talk to the other child!!!

When we make a bad choice in the way we react or the things that we do, it can sometimes be hard to backtrack. Narrative can help us to see a mistake and solve it without having to feel uncomfortable. Jake was able to wake as the puppy, but it would have been harder for him to stand up as himself and go back to his seat. He'd become trapped in the game of pretending to be asleep, and once the audience clapped and he didn't leave the stage, the path home had been closed to him. By becoming cockerels, the children offered him a storyline route back.

If we can help children to find narratives that prepare them for the range of complex emotions they will experience on their journey through life, then we are giving them strategies that will last. We don't have to do this alone. Just listen for the ones that arise from the children and seek wisdom from the group.

I don't know what to do

Several years ago, I ran an introductory session with Grade 1 children from a school in Boston. I started by introducing some stories, and I was impressed with how eagerly these six- and seven-year-olds committed to the acting out. I asked if anyone would like to tell me a story. Logan put his hand up, and I invited him to sit by me so that I could write down his words.

Just as Logan moved to join me, another boy, Tyler, sprang into action, charging to my side. Now I had two boys facing me, eager to tell their story.

'I want to go first', said Tyler.

'She said me', replied Logan.

'Tyler', I said, 'I told Logan that I would take his story. Would you mind going back to your place and I will take a story from you in a minute?'

Tyler looked at me and shook his head. I tried again.

'Tyler, I am happy to take a story from you, but I have just invited Logan to tell his story. I wonder if you would be happy to wait a little while, and I then I will be able to scribe a story from you'.

Tyler shook his head again. He shuffled closer to me and asked Logan if he was going to tell the story about the dragons. Logan nodded and Tyler replied,

'That's my story. I want to tell it'.

I reminded Tyler that I was happy to take his story in a minute. I could see by the look on his face that he wasn't going anywhere. His teacher looked uncomfortable. I wondered if she would drag him out of the way. Neither of us wanted that. Using the fact that I am bigger and can pick children up and move them has never been one of my strategies. I had to face this one out. Then I remembered. I didn't need to have the answer. It was their conflict; let them find the solution.

With renewed confidence I turned to the two boys and said the following:

'I don't know what to do. Logan was here first and is ready to tell his story, but Tyler also wants to tell his story. We have a problem, and I have no idea how to solve it. What do you suggest?'

Logan was the first to reply. 'I could tell half of the story and then Tyler could tell the second half', he said.

I thanked Logan for his idea and asked Tyler if he was happy with it. He shook his head. I then turned to the rest of the class.

'I have a bit of a problem and I don't know what to do'. I reiterated the issue again and reminded the class of the solution Logan had come up with but noted that Tyler wasn't happy with it. Angel put her hand up.

'Maybe Logan could say one line and Tyler could say one line and they could tell the story like that', she suggested.

I asked Tyler his thoughts on the solution and again he shook his head. I summed up where we were with the class, how two suggestions had been made and how I was still unsure what to do as none of the suggestions had worked for Tyler. As I didn't know how to solve the problem I waited to see if there were any more thoughts on a way forward. Then Tyler spoke. 'I'll do what he said'. He pointed to Logan.

Tyler and Logan worked out who was going to tell which half of the story. They even worked with me to draw a line across the middle of the page, so that each of them knew how much space they had for their section.

Logan began.

'There were two dragons'. Looking at Tyler, he added, 'That will be me and you'.

When Tyler took over the story, he continued it seamlessly. This was a story they played regularly. They both knew the characters and the world they inhabited. Perhaps because the story was one they knew so well, they felt a shared ownership of it, and Tyler found it impossible to allow Logan to tell it without him, Whatever the reason, it was not something that has happened to me before or since, but it will stay in my mind as a reminder that the best things occur when I stop looking for solutions and let the children discover them for themselves.

I want to be Batman

On another day, in a classroom in London, I remembered the lessons of Boston and invited the children to help me to solve a problem that was happening for one of the children in their class.

Dafari was upset. He wanted to be Batman in Damian's story, but he was sitting on the other side of the stage and it wasn't his turn. He had already walked up to the teacher and the teaching assistant to ask if he could be Batman, and he had been told to sit back down. I was aware something was happening, but Damian was stood in front of me and was involved in a very intricate description of how Batman flew, which he was sharing with the girl who was playing this role. I was supporting both these children in this negotiation.

Dafari's need to be Batman passed me by. Until he started crying. As soon as I saw this I stopped everything I was doing. However trivial the tears might seem, I am a great believer that if a child is unhappy, then it is my job to listen, to find out what his unmet need is, and to support him in finding a resolution. If we want our children to grow into emotionally intelligent, empathetic individuals, I believe it is vital we take moments like these seriously. I have often been told that a child is just playing up or is using tears to get attention. If a child is upset enough to cry, even if it is 'just to get attention', then knowing he is being listened to will help him to develop the confidence in himself to make different choices next time.

Having stopped the acting out, I asked Dafari what was wrong.

'I want to be Batman', he replied tearfully.

I reminded Dafari that when we do acting out we go around the stage so that everyone has a turn. It would be his turn shortly.

'But I want to be Batman', Dafari cried.

I stopped for a moment. Here was a child, obviously distraught that he was not Batman. What should I do? Everything in me screamed, let him be Batman, and a tiny little part of me went, ahhh haha, maybe he needs to learn to take turns. I'm glad I was able to ignore that part.

'Dafari', I said, 'do you need to be Batman now, or can you wait, and I can take a Batman story from you later, once we have acted out all the other stories?'

'Now', whispered Dafari.

I turned to the other children. 'Dafari is really upset that he didn't get the chance to be Batman in Damien's story. Is it all right if I give him the chance to be Batman now?'

The children agreed. I think they share with me the need to ensure that everyone is listened to. No one wanted to carry on playing when they knew one of their classmates was upset.

When I asked Dafari his story, he said, 'Batman'. It wasn't a long story. He normally told longer. All he wanted was to play that part. He stood on the stage, and I asked him to show me how Batman moved. He took his moment and flew around, and then we all clapped thank you and he returned to his place. We carried on with the other story. Dafari, content that he had been Batman, was happy to wait his turn and joined in for the rest of the morning. The other children, relieved to have seen an act of kindness, carried on as if nothing had happened.

Afterwards, and both at separate times, the teacher and the teaching assistant came up to me. They were amazed that the other children hadn't started to say they wanted to be Batman when I gave Dafari the floor. They asked if it was fair to let one child be Batman, just because he was crying.

All I could answer was that I trusted the kindness of the other children. If a child wanted to be Batman enough to cry about it, then it would feel unkind not to let him have a turn, even if it was a bit early. Isn't this exactly the kind of negotiations that children are engaged in when they play? If this resulted in the unlikely event of all the children crying to be Batman, then I would ask them how to solve this problem. Maybe they would all need to get up and run around as Batman before we engaged in the next story. Who knows? The truth is that I have never found that supporting the needs of the individual has resulted in all the children creating their own fictitious unmet needs just so that I would support them too.

These four-year-olds are learning about turn taking, equality and fairness every day and are basing their understanding of this on the decisions they see the adults around them making. Is treating everyone equally the same as being fair?

Dafari was given a little bit extra on that day because on that day Dafari's needs were a little bit greater. Tomorrow another child might need a little bit more, and maybe Dafari will remember how it felt to be listened to when he was feeling sad. If something upsets a child enough to cry, then surely by dealing with it compassionately we support all our children in growing up to be the caring and emotionally intelligent individuals our world is crying out for.

The day no one said no

As I am often running sessions in new classrooms, I always let the adults in the room know that I am happy to manage the group and that it would be great if they could just sit around the stage and support me but that they don't need to intervene.

Another thing I do when I begin working with new children is that I ask if everyone can wear clearly written name tags so that I can refer to them directly when I am introducing the approach. I have started being more specific about the words 'clearly written' in later years, as sometimes the writing is so small I can hardly read it, and occasionally, when I'm working in a beautifully child-centered nursery, I sit around the stage, only to discover that the staff have invited the children to write their own labels, using their various stages of emergent writing. Although I love the sentiment, it makes it so hard for me to know who I am talking to.

A setting I was working with a while ago had followed my instructions and even remembered to label the children for the second visit. Isla Hill had introduced the approach the week before, and we were now gathered around the stage to act out the stories we had taken throughout the morning. The labels were clearly written and were stuck neatly on the children's chests for all to see. Then one three-year-old boy decided to do what hundreds of children have done before and unpeeled the label and stuck it over his mouth.

But on this day something different happened. The nursery staff we were working with and the two of us from MakeBelieve Arts decided to say nothing.

Another boy followed suit, and we went on with the activity, acting out the Private Stories the children had told us earlier and not really noticing the ever-increasing number of children with sticky labels on their mouths.

I lie; we did notice. All the adults in the room noticed, and most of us probably had twitchy fingers to peel them off. But this was the day that for some reason, without any prior discussion, we had all decided not to say no.

Steven was one of the first stories to be acted out. He sat in front of Isla, ready to begin.

> A dragon came
> > it ate a carrot
> > The dragon ate an orange

A sticker was firmly placed over his mouth, proudly proclaiming his name. When Isla asked, 'Can we see the dragon eating the carrot?' from behind the sticker his mouth moved in a munching fashion, while his hands mimed a scratching movement. He seemed oblivious to the sticker, and so did all the other children. This was just how Steven chose to play the dragon, and everyone in the room accepted it.

There was a division on that day between the children who placed stickers over their mouths and the ones where the stickers were not for them. Both were respectful of the other group, maybe not even aware of what group they were in.

And all the adults in the room, who were very aware of the sticker regime, pretended to be children who weren't bothered by such strange behaviour, and no one said a word.

After the session we gathered, us adults, to talk. And one of the first questions from the nursery staff was, 'Should we have taken the stickers off the children who were putting them over their mouths?' And 'was it right that it bothered us?' They also told us that if we hadn't have been there, maybe they would have stopped it happening. But for some reason, this was the day that all of us decided not to say no.

And the stickers on the mouth didn't hurt or bother the children. It didn't affect their engagement with the activity. And the only people who were even slightly anxious about it were the adults.

And all our discussions made me laugh. I loved that seeing children with stickers over their mouths had made me feel uncomfortable, as if I should have stopped them or made them focus. But I also love that I knew this was my problem and not the children's.

For a little while afterwards, I wondered why, in all the sessions I have done, with all the name labels I have placed on children throughout this time, I had never seen so many labels on mouths as I did that day. Then it dawned on me. On other stickers-on-mouths days, the children have been discouraged; stickers have been taken off, and hands have been gently held down to stop the children from displaying their name across their mouths. I have memories of children told off for being silly or of frowns across the stage, accompanied by the subtle shaking of a head.

But on this day, the day no one said no. We allowed the children who wanted to play the stickers-on-mouth game, and no one was harmed in any way.

Make 'em laugh

I received an e-mail from a teacher who was struggling to relate to the stories that her children were telling.

'Making friends laugh has become the motive for storytelling for some of the children in our preschool class. While entertaining at times, many of these "funny" stories make little sense and render a reaction much like that with slapstick comedies. The audience laughs at the pure silliness of the stories and the, often goofy, performance of its actors.

'Bringing the group together in laugher is fun and the common thread of laughing for the sake of laughing fosters some sense of community among the children. Yet, I find myself questioning the value of stories told mainly for the purpose of eliciting a reaction from the audience'.

This is an extract of one of the stories:

> . . . There was a face potato and then the face potato cross the bridge. And the bridge began to break. And then there was the face potato had no fighting again.
> And then there was a monster potato and then there was 10 potato monsters.

And they walked upside down. And then there was a bucket full water.
And then it went on one of the potato monster's face.
And then there was a . . . then he said, 'No! I'll never fight again!'
And then there was a baby full of water and he was a Lumbo Bee.
It's really big, it's really fat and it's upside down.

This story carried on for a lot longer. My first suggestion was to recommend A5 paper for scribing so that the stories were a standardised maximum length.

Part of the story looked like the child was editing as he went along: 'And then there was a . . . then he said 'No . . .' If I were the scribe I would have waited till he worked out his sentence and then written the words.

I was told that the main authors were dual-language learners, who had become eager to tell stories in English and to act these out in front of their peers. The teacher's frustration was that she wanted her children to tell stories with greater plot and meaning, and she was wondering how to push for this.

This issue of wanting the stories that children tell us to conform to our adult notion of storytelling is not uncommon, and I can empathise with it. Sometimes a child will include an image that is so intriguing that I want to know more about it, but maybe the child is not ready to tell me, or maybe that novel is not ready to be born. All I can do is watch eagerly and see where the child takes it.

In Lucas's story there are some fun images: 'A baby full of water and he was a Lumbo Bee . . . really big, it's really fat and it's upside down'. After he finished his story, I would have asked him to show me how the Lumbo Bee moved when it was upside down or asked about Lumbo Bees. This is not to add to the story but for my own understanding. I suspect his Lumbo bee is a mispronounced Bumble Bee, and further conversations might have revealed this.

I have heard many practitioners express their worries that a child or group of children are being silly or playing the class clown when they act out their stories. When this happens in a session I embrace the silliness. If children start acting in a slapstick manner or falling over a lot, I want to share with them slapstick films or nonsense rhymes to feed their interest.

In Vivian Gussin Paley's classroom, storytelling was the essence of her curriculum. In *The Girl with the Brown Crayon* (1998), Vivian shares with the class the stories of Leo Lionni. In another book she talks about reading 'The Tinderbox'.

If we create stories or tell children classic stories, their repertoire will increase, their understanding of story structure will grow and this will feed into Storytelling and Story Acting. If children like nonsense, pepper these stories-sharing sessions with a diet of rhymes or humorous tales. There are many types of stories in the world, and the more we expose our children to them, the richer their narrative development will be.

8 Shush, don't tell anyone
The big secret

Once upon a time there was a queen.
She didn't had a castle.
Then she saw a castle.
Suddenly a alien came.
Alien was friends. They was playing.
(Esha, age 4)

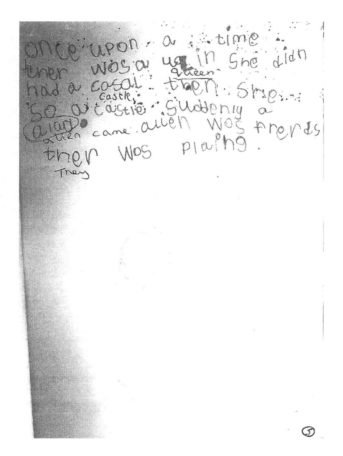

Figure 8.1 Story written by Esha to act out

What I am about to write is a big secret. As you read my words, I hope you will understand the dilemma I face in sharing it with you. There are people, not you I am sure, but those amongst us in education who might take this knowledge and use it improperly.

The following pages carry an early-years health warning

Ever since I first started delivering Helicopter Stories, I became aware that this approach has the ability to encourage children to get excited about writing.

When do children, in today's society, have the opportunity to observe the process of writing? As tablet computers and mobile technologies advance, the need for us to pick up a pen and paper becomes less, limited perhaps to a scribbled note or a shopping list. Once children witness writing on a regular basis, they realise how important it is. These symbols capture their stories. This is much more interesting than the writing the 'teacher' wants them to do.

For many of the children I've worked with, this regular observation of writing for a purpose encourages them to pick up a pen and paper and start to write. This often starts with one or two children who decide they would like to play at taking stories. I have overheard one child asking a friend if she has a story she would like to share. This sometimes catches on, and then others join in, searching for pens and paper so they can record the words of anyone who will talk to them.

There are other times when writing remains the sole occupation of the child who initiated it, or it fizzles out and becomes a short-lived game. But over the 15 years that I have been delivering Helicopter Stories, it has happened enough for me to know that this is an unsung benefit of the approach.

So why, with such a fantastic early literacy possibility arising from this work, am I so adamant that the examples I am about to include carry an Early-Years Health Warning?

In the current climate, despite all the evidence to the contrary, many government education departments across the world are losing sight of the value of fantasy play in children's lives.

In the UK, with its increased emphasis on base-line testing, the pressures on early-years settings to develop the 'school readiness' of young children and a climate that places academic skills above confidence, independence and curiosity, I worry that a programme that engages children in writing because they choose to could so easily become a way of getting children writing because they have to.

The writing that happens as a by-product of Storytelling and Story Acting is a result of how this approach respects children's need to explore the world in the way they choose. I would hate for engagement with early writing to be seen as one of the outputs of this approach. If children get excited about writing because of Helicopter Stories, that is fantastic. If they don't, it doesn't matter. They are still learning loads about the process of writing, how it looks on the page, where the spaces are, which direction the writing goes, and all of this just from watching what is happening whilst their story is scribed. No teaching required.

Connor, age 4

The first time I realised that Helicopter Stories engage children with writing was in 2000, in a school in Southwark.

I was taking stories from Blue Class when Connor walked past with a pen and paper in his hand. He was on my list to tell a story, so I called out to him and asked if he was ready.

Figure 8.2 Connor writing

'I don't need to tell you a story, I'm writing me myself', Connor replied.

He sat down near me, and as I scribed a story from another of his classmates, he happily filled an A4 sheet with emergent writing. His teacher, who was standing nearby, looked at me with open mouth. Connor never went near the drawing table. She had never seen him work in this way, and for a moment both of us watched him, engrossed in creating his characters, unaware of our attention. His writing finished, he ran off, leaving the paper on the table. I still have a photocopy of it today and the Post-It note that the teacher wrote to accompany it.

The day I didn't scribe stories

Different versions of the example just presented have happened many times over the years, where I have witnessed children deciding to write their own story or pretending to be me and play at scribing with other children. But one day, a few years ago, the quantity of writing that occurred surprised me.

I was working in two classes in a setting in Tower Hamlets, one of the poorest boroughs in London. While I was scribing the stories from one class, four-year-old Esha, whose story appears at the top of this chapter, asked if it was okay to act out a story she had written at home. I agreed. Esha was in the other group, so I told her that I would be with her class in a little while, once I had finished acting out the stories I'd taken from the first class.

Half an hour later I walked over to Esha's classroom and was greeted by her teacher, who was looking at me in a perplexed manner. In her hand was a wad of papers. Written on every one of them was a story from a child aged between three and five years old. There were 13 stories in all. The teacher told me that once Esha had spoken to me, she returned to the room and started telling everyone that I was going to let her act out in a story she had written herself. One of her friends replied that she wanted to write a story to be acted out, and then another, and another. Thirteen children out of a class of 22 wrote their stories, without any prompting from the adults in the room.

This is one of the stories. It's from a three-year-old boy who had recently been in hospital. The teacher asked him to tell her the story of his writing as he was adamant that it was to be acted out. As he dictated it to her, he pointed to parts of the writing, mirroring the way that I read back a story to the child.

Figure 8.3 Injection story

Typing versus handwriting

In recent years there has been some debate around whether typing stories rather than scribing them by hand has an impact on this activity.

At first I was open to the idea of typing, thinking that maybe, for younger practitioners, the ease with which they typed and the ease with which children accessed content in the digital age might produce interesting results. Choosing not to judge something before I had seen it, I asked a teacher who was regularly typing children's dictated stories if she could show me how it worked.

As I watched her typing, I was surprised at how distant the boy whose story she was recording seemed to be from the process of what was happening on the screen. He spoke his words, and the teacher typed them. There was none of the connections between the words and the action of writing that I see children making when I scribe. The boy looked in the air as he spoke; he stood in front of her, with the back of her laptop between them, and the intimacy, that for me is a part of Storytelling and Story Acting was missing.

The teacher had made provisions for engaging children with print recognition by choosing a large font size, but as we talked, it became obvious that none of this made any difference. Children rarely looked at the screen when their stories were typed, regardless of how large the writing was.

In 2013, during a series of e-mailed conversations among Patsy Cooper, Gillian McNamee, Jane Katch and myself, the four of us discussed this issue. The unanimous feeling was that writing by hand was far more beneficial than typing.

Patsy Cooper shared her experiences of disseminating the approach in Houston.

> I've traced the progression of storytellers from age two to the age when they read and write on their own (say kindergarten or first grade) in terms of their body language. The findings tell us that young children have to discover, constructivist-style that the words come from their mouths to the scribe's head to the pencil to the paper. In brief, pictorially-speaking, new two-year-old storytellers tell to the air, and are only happy to discover during dramatization their words showed up on the paper, too.
>
> At three, they tell you to 'write that down,' aware that something important is happening on that paper, and that they are somehow in charge. At four, their faces get close and closer to the paper as they monitor your speed and accuracy. Versions of 'Did you get that?' or 'Where did you write that?' or 'See, teacher, there's more room over here' (pointing to the margin) are often heard. Mature storytellers, however, sit back and just dictate, like the boss to the secretary, confident of how words get from their heads to the paper, and happy to concentrate on the story's details.
>
> Here's the interesting thing: We saw no such discovery or attempt to control print in the children from classes where teachers insisted they would only take dictation if they could use a computer. And so we now don't accept teachers into the training program who won't scribe without it.

The benefits that Patsy outlines convince me that this activity must be scribed manually.

There are plenty of opportunities in our settings where technology can be used, but Storytelling and Story Acting is not one of them. I have heard several justifications for typing, including how convenient it is for the teacher, enabling them publish the stories later or share them with the parents. But this approach is a live experience, an instant process of telling stories and acting them out. If parents want to see a copy, I have always found a photocopier to be the easiest way of sharing the handwritten word.

> For as long as children learn to write by hand, I believe this is the way to write their stories. We've probably all seen children, like the ones Trish showed us, who learned to 'write' their own stories, copying our scribing process. We've seen kids learn their own invented spelling because they couldn't wait for their turn at the Story Table. How can they copy us and learn to do this if we use a keyboard? Of course there may be a special reason to type them from time to time – maybe there's a parent night coming up and you want the stories more legible, displayed on the wall. Or you want to type a copy of each child's favourite story for an end-of-year collection. But for the daily storytelling, why wouldn't we want to do it in the way we want the children to learn to write?
>
> (Jane Katch)

> All learning as we know is sensorimotor in the beginning – it is physical, it needs to be tangible, it is powerful when we get our hands on it. For children's hands and brain development, we want their hands to manipulate a pencil and get their hands on paper. We want them to watch every line and mark the scribe makes on paper, and to enjoy the physical-ness of it, hearing the teacher echo each sound as he or she makes the word. Printing in big letters illustrates the making of a word in a way that typing cannot do.
>
> (Gillian McNamee)

If we want children to learn to write, we need to model the process of writing. When children see us writing for a purpose, the purpose of catching their words on the page so that we can support them to represent these in action, writing grows in status.

When writing has a purpose, children may start to attempt it themselves, but remember, this is not the aim of Helicopter Stories, just a happy by-product.

Fiona, age 4

In a setting in Kent, a four-year-old girl sat at a table. It was the day my colleague Isla Hill was working with the class, and everyone was getting settled for a morning of Helicopter. As Isla took off her coat and got ready to scribe her first story, she overheard Fiona speaking to a group of children.

'I'm going to be taking stories today'.

A boy, John, sat next to her, and Fiona, taking a pen and paper from the other side of the table, looked at him and asked, 'Would you like to tell me a story?' John nodded. What happened next was videoed and is a transcript of the actual words and actions used by both children.

Fiona was confident writing the letter F. As she took on the role of scribe, she also repeated back to John, writing a letter F for each word he spoke, in some cases, writing this letter several times, breaking down each syllable. It is hard to remember that Fiona is four years old when you read the transcript, but here is a child in the early years, mirroring the practice she has seen performed by the adults in the room and scribing a story with the use of just one letter.

JOHN: There's a little doggy that had a wolf in his belly.
(Fiona repeats his words as she writes, always using the letter F and leaning in to look at John to ensure she has captured him correctly.)

FIONA: (writing) There's a little doggy that?
JOHN: Has a wolf in his belly,
FIONA: A wolf in his belly?
JOHN: Yes.
FIONA: (writing) had a wolf in his belly . . .
         What happened next?
JOHN: The wolf came out and he smashed the wolf in his window.
FIONA: The wolf came?
JOHN: Out,
FIONA: (writing) and?
JOHN: and he smashed,
FIONA: (writing) and he?
JOHN: smashed the wolf out,
FIONA: (writing) and he then smashed the?
JOHN: wolf out the window.
FIONA: (writing) the wolf out his window.
JOHN: And the wolf was born.
FIONA: (writing) And the wolf was born.
JOHN: Then he smashed a eyeball from a wolf.
FIONA: (writing) Then he smashed a eyeball from the wolf.
JOHN: Then he smashed in his belly.
FIONA: (writing) Then he smashed in his belly.
(Fiona starts to get restless, looking around a bit more, but continues to scribe.)
JOHN: Then he died.
FIONA: (writing) Then he died (said as if the end of a story).
JOHN: When he was born he died in a tree.
FIONA: When he was born he died in a? tree?
(Fiona gets more restless as she questions John.)
JOHN: tree,
FIONA: (writing) tree,
JOHN: and when he was born he got out of the tree and then he went in the eyeball.
FIONA: (writing) and when he was born he got out of the tree and . . .
JOHN: He went in the eyeball and he smashed it with his eye.
FIONA: (writing) and he went in the eyeball. He smashed it with his eye.
JOHN: And when he got out of it, he smashed it with a knife.
FIONA: And when he got out of it he?
JOHN: smashed it with a knife,
FIONA: (writing) smashed it with a knife.
JOHN: and when he got out of it then he was born.
FIONA: I think it should be the end now (smiling kindly at John).
JOHN: Okay.
FIONA: (writing) The End.

When it was time for the acting out, Isla was handed a piece of paper covered with the letter F. Unable to read it, she asked Fiona if she would like to lead this part of the session. Together, with Isla's and John's help, Fiona recalled the story fairly accurately, inviting other children onto the stage to take on the various roles necessary to bring the story to life.

Figure 8.4 Fiona writing

Source: Cremin et al 2013: 74.

The detail and concentration required by Fiona to scribe for such an extended period was incredible, as was the fact that, having written the story, she was also able to recall several of the key details without prompting. The film clip of her scribing lasts nearly five minutes, and during that time Fiona continues to write the letter F to correspond with each of John's word. She works hard to understand and record exactly what John is saying.

Would Fiona have done this if the stories she'd seen scribed had been typed on a laptop?

> If we don't model what we teach, we are teaching something else.
>
> (Abraham Maslow)

The learning children experience from having their story handwritten is evidenced in all the examples I have presented.

I sometimes wonder if in the future we will discover emergent typing, as children get more exposure to digital technology. I have seen videos of babies pressing on a photo of a magazine, trying to get it to digitally change pages. We have no idea what the effects of increased access to technology will be on the very young. This will be uncovered only as the twenty-first century emerges.

However, for now, my experience shows me that the secret benefit of Storytelling and Story Acting happens only because children are exposed to an approach that demonstrates the value and the potential of the written word. If we want children to write, they have to see us writing.

But remember, shush, don't tell anyone . . .

9 She Bumped, and she Pow, and she landed, Bang
To scaffold or to model?

Once upon a time there was a princess, and there was Snow White.
And Cinderella was a princess that was running, and she fell down.
She Bumped, and she Pow and she landed, Bang.
And she went home to have a drink, and she went to the doctors.
And she had a necklace, and she falled on it.
And she Bang again.

(Rebecca, age 4)

The poetry of children

When children dictate their stories to me, I find myself fascinated by the order of their words and the effect this has on the rhythm and poetic quality of their narrative. The story above is no exception. The phrase 'Cinderella was a princess that was running' gives a weight to the story that would not be present if an adult had told a similar tale. In Standard English we would write, 'Princess Cinderella was running' or even 'Cinderella, the princess, was running'.

Rebecca's choice of word order places a different emphasis on her story. 'Cinderella was a princess that was running'. She presents a princess who needed to run. Her phrasing accentuates the word 'princess,' suggesting an underlying premise behind the act of running, and the fact that the person doing it is royalty. Perhaps princesses aren't allowed to run in this kingdom, or maybe they don't usually run. Rebecca makes us believe that a princess running is out of the ordinary.

Given the suggestion that running is unusual, it is hardly surprising that in the next sentence the princess falls over. This allows Rebecca to demonstrate her knowledge of story language, as she describes the event. 'She Bumped, and she Pow, and she landed, Bang'. If this sentence appeared in a children's picture book, we would readily accept that its author was an adult. The words might have been borrowed from another story, but there was something in the way Rebecca delivered these lines that demonstrated her love of wordplay.

Made-up words

I find great pleasure, as I scribe children's stories, in the words they sometimes invent when the correct one is unknown to them.

Once upon a time there was a girl, and the girl was very married.
And she danced to the music with her marrier.

And then there was big bad wolf sneaking while she was dancing.

And then they looked behind them and then they saw a wolf and the wolf gobbled them up.

And then they was alive again.

And they went home and then they saw a broken chair.

So much they liked the broken chair, it broked into little pieces.

And they then sitted on their new settee.

(Bethany, age 4)

If a person who bakes bread is a baker and a person who teaches is a teacher, then how beautifully creative and absolutely logical for a person you marry to become your 'marrier'.

The idea of a girl dancing to the music with her 'marrier' is one of the most romantic images I have ever heard. I find myself wanting to dance along. Who wants a husband or a wife when you can have a 'marrier' to dance with? Of course, there is always the big bad wolf sneaking up on you, waiting to gobble you up, but the author allows us to come alive again, to watch as the broken chair, that 'so much we like', breaks even further and results in us sitting on our new settee.

Bethany plays with grammar. She is four years old and is full of stories and narrative word play. Storytelling and Story Acting offers a place where she can record her tales without needing to make changes or corrections. This allows her words to shine through.

Similes

The police catch the princess.

The dragon takes the police.

And towns are getting fired.

And the police office and the bus people fighting.

And the police jacket, and the princess jacket and the bus people jacket getting fired.

And every police car fired.

It must be dragon, blowing fire, and fire engine squeezing water like a fish.

(Sarjot, age 3)

Sarjot's story starts with rhythmic poetry. In the fifth sentence, he incorporates the rule of three (the story principal which suggest that things that come in threes are inherently more satisfying). I doubt Sarjot has studied this rule, but I can tell he has been exposed to enough stories for this rhythm to become instinctive.

When we reach the final sentence we are greeted by a simile, 'fire engine squeezing water like a fish'. It's not a clichéd. It's not a phrase I've ever come across, but as an image that captures the way the fire engines are squirting water onto the fire, it works. I can picture the hose, looking like a fish's mouth, and water being pushed out of it in spurts. It's possibly not the best way to put out a fire, but I can imagine it and empathise with the difficulties of the task.

It also makes me wonder how a three-year-old imagined this. What images and thoughts collided to enable these words to pour effortlessly from his mouth?

It is in these moments that I glimpse the truth about this thing we call story and the way it enables us to tap into something beyond conscious thought.

The motive behind scribing verbatim

Before I begin this section, it would be wrong not to mention the debate over whether it is better to scribe verbatim or to correct the grammar or prompt for more information when recording children's stories. At MakeBelieve Arts, during Helicopter Stories, we scribe exactly, whatever the child dictates. Other approaches to Storytelling and Story Acting have made different choices.

In an e-mail correspondence I had with Patsy Cooper, she sums up the difference in these methods:

> Some children are more fluent in non-standard English than standard usage. The one-on-one nature of the dictation process allows teachers to address this as they see fit. Teachers I work with usually take one of three routes.
>
> - The first group write down exactly what the child says. The idea is that the child will adopt standard speech when he or she is ready.
> - The second calls the child's attention to the deviation from Standard English, suggests the standard form, and requests permission to write it that way. Sometimes the children give permission, sometimes they do not.
> - The third group echoes what the child says, but with modification from non-standard to standard, much like what many mothers do to correct children's speech. If the child does not object, the teacher proceeds to write it down in the modified form.
>
> The point is that in all three instances, dictation offers teachers a chance to teach the children about language usage, and to learn what the children know, or are ready to know. There is no one way to approach this issue.

I am regularly asked about the rationale behind scribing word for word. For me a big part of my answer is outlined here; the other part is my appreciation of the poetic language I hear in children's speech.

Often magazines share the quirky things that children say, finding humour in their insights about a world that is alien to them. These are seen as cute anecdotes, but the observations or the sometimes unorthodox approach to word order can be highly intuitive. The fact that we engage with them so readily is surely testament to the way they connect with us on some unconscious level.

Imagine how fantastic the literature of future generations would be if children were able to maintain some degree of creativity and improvisation with their language usage, alongside their lessons in grammar and sentence structure.

I know how hard it is to value creativity in this age of testing and the results-driven focus in education. Trusting that children will find their way if you scribe for them verbatim can feel risky when OFSTED is due. Government policies on driving up teaching standards can so easily trap us in a culture of fear and result in our undervaluing the very tools children use to engage with learning.

> The children themselves continually reminded us that play was still their most usable context. It was not the monsters they invented that frightened them in kindergarten, it was being told to sit still and pay attention for long periods of time.
>
> (Paley 2004)

When I am scribing Helicopter Stories, I think of it primarily as a creative activity. I am writing down exactly what the children say and celebrating the words and language they use to express themselves. I also see the hidden teaching and learning benefits that are contained within this approach.

From the perspective of knowing the group, there is an advantage of having a record of the exact language children are using at any given moment. As I date all the stories, I have documentation showing how an individual or the whole class have developed over a longer period of time. Are they still incorporating the same themes as they did when the project started? Have they begun to tell longer stories? How have their stories changed? Are the individual stories influenced by the themes within the classroom? I also have fantastic evidence of language development within the group, alongside an understanding of where there are difficulties. My verbatim stories are filled with information that can inform the work of other areas of the classroom.

Types of questions

In Chapter 3, I describe the type of clarifying questions I might ask when I have finished scribing a story. How many princess are there? When you said 'he ran away', did you mean the superman ran away or the baddy? These are production questions, which help me to stage manage the acting out. They shape my understanding and assist me in helping to realise the author's vision.

If I asked these questions while I was scribing, it might break the momentum. This is not always the case; sometimes, as in the example that follows, the desire to tell the story is such that the child will continue with great persistence, even when the scribe bombards her with queries. However, as you can see, at the end of this story the child runs out of steam.

Interrupting dictation

The script below is a true account of what happened between a four-year-old and her teacher. It was scribed verbatim during a visit to a setting.

TEACHER: Have you got a story for me?
CHILD: Yes, a gingerbread man run.
TEACHER: I'm sorry was that run or ran?
CHILD: Run A . . . Cross.
TEACHER: No, 'across' is one word.
CHILD: The street and the gingerbread man saw a cow, and the cow said.
TEACHER: Quotation marks, the cow's going to talk!
CHILD: 'Can you stop running' said the cow? Then he saw a police.
TEACHER: A police or the police?
CHILD: A police, and the police said 'I'm getting hungry'. He want . . .
TEACHER: Want or wanted?
CHILD: Wanted to eat the gingerbread man and he saw a fox and then she saw a river. That's the end.
TEACHER: That's the end? But we've got lots more room. What happened next?
CHILD: And the fox said 'climb on his'.
TEACHER: Climb on his, or climb on my?
CHILD: Climb on my tail. It getting . . .
TEACHER: It or it's?

CHILD: It's getting closer to the bottom.
TEACHER: He said that or the fox said that?
CHILD: The gingerbread man said that. So the gingerbread man climb.
TEACHER: Climb or climbed.
CHILD: Climb onto the fox back.
TEACHER: Fox or fox's.
CHILD: Fox's back and then it was getting closer and closer.
TEACHER: I like the way you said that with the expression.
CHILD: So the fox say.
TEACHER: Say or said.
CHILD: Said 'climb on my nose'. The end.
TEACHER: And then? Did he eat it? You want to end it right there?
CHILD: Yes (adamantly).

The teacher's objective – to ensure that the child spoke in Standard English – got in the way of her appreciation of the poetry of the story. Only at one point did she remark on it, and by then the praise was buried in a sea of other questions.

> Though fantasy propels the child to poetic heights over and above his ordinary level and was considered the original pathway to literacy, it is now perceived by some as an obstacle to learning. We are allowed to nourish play only so long as it initiates reading, writing and computing. We continue to call play the work of young children, whilst reducing its appearance to brief interludes.
>
> (Paley 2004)

Grammar

As we have seen in many of the examples throughout this book, when children develop communication skills, they often produce words that are grammatically incorrect. Often they add an extra 'ed' sounds onto the ends of words. Correctly used, 'walk' becomes 'walked', 'talk' becomes 'talked', but incorrectly, yet following the same rule, 'sleep' becomes 'sleeped' and 'creep' becomes 'creeped'.

Steven Pinker, in his book *The Language Instinct* (1994), writes:

> The errors children make are rarely random garbage. Often they follow the logic of grammar so beautifully that the puzzle is not why the children make the errors, but why they sound like errors to the adult ears at all.

Pinker argues that following these grammatical rules is part of an innate language instinct that comes before a child learns all the irregular verbs and exceptional grammatical rules that form so much of our English language.

Finding the logic

In this example, Arek readily engages with storytelling even though he had arrived in London only a few weeks previously. His first language is Polish, but even with his limited English the narrative he is trying to convey is clear.

> Boy got car, it fast, it go wicked. Bruuummmm . . .
>
> (Arek, age 4)

When the story was acted out, the gasps of wonder from the group at the phrase 'it go wicked' demonstrated the connection the children made with the language Arek used. Not one child said, 'What do you mean? "It go wicked", that doesn't make sense. I don't understand'. The children readily accepted the phrase, and joined with the boy in charging around the stage.

These are phrases that I do not have the skill to correct. If I replaced 'it go wicked' with 'the car went fast,' I would lose the essence of Arek's story. But when I closed my book, I had a fantastic conversation with him about how fast was wicked, which he demonstrated for me, charging around in a circle until he tumbled to the ground.

Talking or reading

Although I scribe and read back the children's words verbatim, when I lead the acting out I always model correct grammar.

> There was a dragon. Then the dragon eat a rat and the dragon died.
>   Then there was a giant. The giant go'ed into the cave.
>   The cave was maked out of stone.
>
> (Malika, age 4)

During the acting out, I read the story exactly as it was written: 'The dragon eat a rat'. Then I ask the child if I can see how the dragon *ate* the rat. Likewise with 'The giant go'ed into the cave', where I asked, 'Can I see the giant going into the cave?' For the sentence 'The cave was maked out of stone' I read exactly what was written, but during the acting out I asked if I could see how the relevant actor would pretend to be a cave *made* out of stone.

This incorporation of verbatim scribing alongside modelling correct grammatical structures in speech is to me a vital part of this approach and the way that I see this work supporting language acquisition.

> Young children, who are still developing their language, are playing with sound, rhythm, syntax and grammar and Helicopter Stories does an effective job of positive cross fertilisation.
>
> (Open University Helicopter Evaluation)

Scaffolding

The term 'scaffolding' was first introduced by Wood, Bruner and Ross (1976) and likens the process of building concepts or skills within a child to the temporary structure that supports the construction of a house. Their idea is based on a Vygotskian concept of the expert supporting the novice.

There is a lot of debate within the field of Storytelling and Story Acting as to whether adults should be supporting children's story development by scaffolding their learning. Scaffolding might involve asking questions during dictation to probe deeper into the story. It could include asking why or what happened next or even requesting more information on a character or an action.

For me, this approach, whilst I am scribing stories, is not how I want to work. I prefer recording the stories exactly as they are and saving all questions and curiosities until after the story is done.

I appreciate expert-novice relationships, but I guess my first question is always, who is the expert? My second would be, which area of expertise are we seeking? Is the purpose of scaffolding to help the child develop his story further? Over a period of several weeks I have watched many children return to their stories, unprompted, to retell and amend certain aspects of them, adding new details and formulating their ideas.

When I am told stories by children and they share with me their world, I sit cross-legged in front of them and readily take my place as the novice, willingly learning their wisdom.

If I were teaching A is for Apple and B is for Bear this relationship might change, but for me it is the extent that the adults and the children in a classroom continually shift from a position of expert to a position of novice that makes learning a dynamic and lifelong activity.

> In dramatic play, language becomes more vivid and spontaneous, enabling young children to connect, with greater fluency and curiosity, the words and phrases they know, to new ideas. The process involves not only the flow of words and imagery, but of shared myth and metaphor, of knowing where the lost babies are and whether a dad can have sharp teeth like a wolf. 'B is for Bear' will teach the letter B, a good thing to know, but one must also know who likes to 'be' the father bear and how bears and kittens might get across a poison river.
>
> (Paley 2004)

Modelling storytelling

If we want Storytelling and Story Acting to thrive in our classroom, we also need to model crafting our own stories or retelling known stories and inviting the children to act these out.

Neuroscience shows us that if we want to engage with something, we need to be emotionally stimulated by it. 'Cells that fire together, wire together', according to Hebb (for more on Hebbian theory, see www.neurohackers.com). Our brains are constantly receiving and processing words and symbols and storing the things that are important to us, that connect with us on an emotional level. If our classrooms are rich in stories, told both by the children and to the children, then the quantity of engaging language they have access to will increase, alongside their confidence in their ability use it.

The more exposure children have to a vast range of stories, the more we develop their ability to make sense of the world through story form.

In *All Our Futures* (1999), a report from the National Advisory Committee on Creativity and Cultural Education, Raymond Williams states, 'to communicate through arts is to convey an experience to others in such a form that the experience is actively recreated, actively lived through by those to whom it is offered'. The report defines the arts as a unique expression of our human perception and feeling: 'if we block it, it will never exist'.

The report goes on to stress how success in one area can go on to stimulate self-esteem and encourage success in others.

> 'Creeped downstairs' comes from Ira. Every year certain phrases are planted and take root, the shoots continually coming up in stories and in play . . . The use of a communal symbol is as tangible a demonstration of socialization as the agreement to share blocks

and dolls . . . 'Creeped downstairs' is a literary and a cultural event . . . Each group chooses its own cultural banners.

(Paley 1990)

By accepting the child's language as it is told, we place value on what they are saying and gain access to the 'cultural banners' each group of storytellers choose to display. In this way we bear witness to the incredible learning potential that surrounds children engaged in fantasy play.

10 Onwards and upwards
Adapting Storytelling and Story Acting to new audiences

Once upon a time there were two frogs. The two frogs were hungry.

So they went to hunt for food. They went to the jungle. In the jungle there was a dark place. So the first frog went inside, and the other one went inside.

The other one was very afraid because it was too dark. And they saw a bunch of bananas. And they took it, and they went back to where they live to share the bananas with the other frogs.

(Ayabuleb, age 9)

Over the years of delivering Helicopter Stories, I have found that one of the most exciting things has been finding out about various derivations that arise as a result of Vivian Gussin Paley's approach. Some of the ones listed in this chapter have come directly through programmes that MakeBelieve Arts has been involved in, but others come from people inspired by Paley who have found ways to adapt Storytelling and Story Acting and make it relevant to the environment they work in.

Year 3 and Year 5, where the learning flows upwards

I have always been a believer in politics being most effective when it comes from the grass roots and flows upwards. Then I realised that this can also be true with learning.

In 2004 I worked with Isla Hill in a primary school in Lewisham, where we were trialling the benefits of Helicopter Stories with two classes of children, one group of Year 3s and one group of Year 5s. Isla worked with the younger age group, and I worked with the older children.

During the tea break of the first day, following a morning of scribing, I met up with a cheerful Isla, whose session had been filled with stories of dragons, trolls and precious stones. I looked at her jealously. My nine- and ten-year-olds had also been dictating stories, but their narratives lacked the richness and imagination of the ones Isla was sharing.

All of my stories were filled with lists of children who were meeting to play a game of football. It was as if they were avoiding the subject of what would happened in the game and instead choosing to names the people who were involved.

Mark and John went to the park and met up with Andrew and Seth. Then Gray and Addi came along. Mustipha and Jason were next, they came with Neo and Jack . . .

After six stories in a similar vein, I was quietly climbing the walls.

As I know from my theatre background, one of the lessons in improvisation is not to run away from the monster but to face it, for that is where the most interesting things happen. I remember wondering whether there was some monster these children were running away from. It was as if whatever they were going to do when they got to the park was bigger than their power to explain it, and so they decided to gather but never partake.

Although I had spent the morning smiling, I was secretly bored, and I didn't know how I would survive six weeks of this. I confided in Isla, and she had a fantastic idea.

After the break I borrowed half of her class and she borrowed half of mine. When we did the acting out, we both had a selection of stories from the younger age group and a selection of stories from the older age group.

Then an incredible thing happened. My nine- and ten-year-olds sat up a little bit straighter when they listened to the stories of the seven- and eight-year-olds in the room. They freed up a lot, happy to pretend to be dragons or castles for this younger audience. By lunchtime I was excited with the transformation, and Isla's experience had been similar. We decided to keep working in this way and see what happened.

The following week, as I began scribing stories, my Year 5 children asked if we were going to do Story Acting with the younger children again. When I said yes they became very excited, and throughout the morning I noticed that the stories they were telling changed. They began to incorporate some of the trolls and dragons that had populated the stories of the Year 3s the previous week. They readily confronted their monsters, fought them and ran home. The teacher couldn't believe the level of their creativity.

Over the following weeks I watched the learning flowing from the bottom up, the younger children reminding the older ones how to tell stories, how to engage in fantasy play and how to confront their monsters. It was as if the older children had forgotten all their instincts about story. Spending time with a group of children where storytelling was very much alive was far more effective than my pushing and prompting them to make their stories more 'interesting'.

By the end of the six weeks, it was hard to tell which stories came from which age group. All the children involved had developed their strengths as storytellers and their sense of community as a shared classroom.

Year 2s scribing for themselves

When Isla Hill worked one day a week for the duration of a year with a class of Year 2 children, she decided to incorporate Storytelling and Story Acting in her curriculum with these rising seven-year-olds. Under pressure to develop their writing skills, Isla wondered if it would be possible to engage the children in scribing stories.

There were 24 children in the class, and on a weekly basis 6 of them paired up and scribed stories from each other. At the end of the day the group acted these out. Isla offered some support to the children during the final session, but the key criterion was that they needed to be able to make sense of their writing, as they were in charge of leading the acting out.

Many of the children struggled with literacy, but Isla was amazed at how readily they engaged in it when they were scribing the story of their partners. Because the person dictating didn't have to worry about how to spell anything, the language was richer and more imaginative. Isla agreed that the books the children wrote in would never be marked. This enabled the scribes to take risks, having a go at spelling words they would normally avoid. They attempted words like 'wonderful' when in their own writing they would stick to the word 'nice'.

Isla firmly believes that the acting out of this activity was paramount. It gave the Year 2s a purpose for their writing, and over the year this fed into other areas of their learning.

Peer-group education

When I first started MakeBelieve Arts I spent a lot of time delivering Helicopter Stories and training practitioners in how to support children using this approach. The more team teaching I did, the more I realised how hard it was for some people to really listen to children in the way this approach demands. Some adults grow inpatient when a child takes a long time to tell her story. Others get bored of the themes that regularly come up, wishing their class would stop telling stories about thunderbirds or Ninja Turtles or whatever the latest hero was at the time. Sometimes the curiosity to see what happened was not there. And it got me thinking.

I began to wonder how children in Year 6 would cope if I trained them as scribes for nursery and reception classrooms. I managed to acquire funding from the Lewisham-based Creating Success, and with permission from Myatt Garden Primary School I set about working with a group of 16 Year 6 pupils, supporting them in much the same way as I would adults, to enable them to deliver Helicopter Stories with younger children. Although I was training the Year 6s, they taught me so much along the way.

What really impressed me was how unhurried the Year 6 children were when they worked with the three- to five-year-olds. They were happy to wait for the younger children to tell their stories, giving them the space and time they needed without any guidance from me.

I watched one 11-year-old boy, Nareem, waiting patiently for five minutes while a 4-year-old sat drinking his milk and not speaking. The two boys showed no impatience with each other, and once the drink was finished Nareem smiled at the boy and asked again if he was ready to tell his story. I am sure that if an adult had been scribing, the cup would have been taken and the boy would have been encouraged to start storytelling and drink later.

Another thing I noticed was how patient the younger children were with the older children. When Rebecca was scribing a story for three-year-old Jai, her pen ran out of ink. She scrambled for another pen, and that one was also not working. Finally she found one that worked, and Jai carried on with his story, paying no attention to the gap.

Some of the Year 6 children struggled with literacy, but they enjoyed recording stories. They realised that the younger children couldn't read what they wrote, and there was no judgement made on their handwriting or spelling. This freed them up. One of the key benefits for older children was the rise in confidence in their writing. Their teacher linked this directly to how Helicopter Stories gave writing a purpose.

One of the reception children was a selective mute, who had not spoken to any adult since he'd started the previous year. One day I noticed him happily telling one of the Year 6 children his story. Similarly, several younger children who whispered their stories to adult scribes were observed speaking much more loudly to the older children, keen to ensure their voices were heard.

When the Year 6 children lacked confidence with leading the acting out, the nursery and reception children seemed to become more confident with their acting. They filled in the gaps, accepting the quieter voice of these older peers whilst doing their best to understand what was asked of them.

Year 6 children would often invite more children onto the stage than I would. They weren't fazed by the chaos. As a result I witnessed the whole class become animals in a story dictated by a three-year-old. I would have cleared the stage several time or found strategies to ensure order. Watching the Year 6 approach, I realised that most children stay in role, even when all around them seems to be in mayhem.

The greatest success for the Peer Group Education approach happened when we rolled it out to Brockley primary school. They invested in the work over a three-year period. Initially we trained a group of Year 5 pupils, who delivered Helicopter Stories one morning a week, throughout the year, supported by a teaching assistant.

When these children moved to Year 6, they were responsible for training a new group of Year 5 pupils, who continued to deliver the approach for another year. This went on for three successive years, with very little support from MakeBelieve Arts. The programme stopped eventually when changes in teaching made it difficult to continue. Until that point, teachers in both the early years and Year 5 commented on the benefits it gave children, developing their literacy, confidence and storytelling abilities.

Storytelling across the ocean

Having made connections with a school in Boston that was regularly engaged in Storytelling and Story Acting, I wondered if it would be possible to share stories across the ocean via Skype.

My interest in this coincided with the launch of the MakeBelieve Arts Helicopter Stories evaluation by the Open University, and so it was decided to explore cross-cultural storytelling in front of a live audience.

When the day arrived, children from the Boston school gathered around a taped-out stage in front of a Skype camera, and children from a school in Tower Hamlets did the same. The time difference only just worked, it was 9.30 a.m. in the morning for them and 2.30 p.m. in the afternoon for us.

We waved hello, and the children in the UK acted out a story that one of them had told previously. They were watched by the live audience in London and by the Skype audience in Boston. Next the American children acted out their story, watched via the whiteboard by our audience. Finally, we acted out a shared story, told by a boy from London:

> Once upon a time there was Spiderman and there was Hulk and then Superman came. And then they found a treasure. Then they put it in the Bat Cave and then Superman took the treasure out of the Bat Cave and gave it to Batman. Batman was taking it in to the Master. Then the Master gave it to the Queen who put it in the locker so no one can get it.

The children in the UK began the process of acting it out, taking on the role of Spiderman, the Hulk and Superman. They found the treasure and placed it carefully in the Bat Cave.

When Superman took the treasure out of the Bat Cave, he handed it to Batman. For the purpose of our acting, Batman was one of the children in Boston. So a child from London handed the treasure through the camera for an American Batman to give to the Master, to hand to the Queen to store in a locker. The moment when the child playing Batman took the treasure through the computer screen was quite incredible.

Skype Storytelling and Story Acting has happened only a few times, but it offers the potential for children to share their stories and to act them out across continents or counties or even between local schools.

Figure 10.1 Boston Skype

Helicopter at Home

Throughout our work at MakeBelieve Arts we have lots of conversations about the importance of engaging parents in the activities of their children, particularly once they enter nursery or reception.

We started working with groups of parents in 2007 by engaging them in creating their own stories that they acted in front of their children. On the day of the sharing, children demonstrated Helicopter Stories so that both groups could see how the other worked.

In 2012 Isla Hill took charge of the programme, and Helicopter at Home was born. Isla wanted to develop the relationship further. She structured a programme of training that started with parents watching their children in Helicopter Stories and then signing up to attend a series of three weekly sessions, where they practiced the approach with each other.

During Helicopter at Home, workshop leaders talk about the benefits of Storytelling and Story Acting on children's learning. Isla encourages parents attending the training to record children's stories at home and bring them back to share with the group. They also look at various methods of recording, using a mobile phone or pen and paper or even just talking stories on the way to school.

Helicopter at Home gives parents a record of the stories their child tells whilst they are growing up. It encourages them to take a role in these, and it creates a link between home and school. In one setting a parent became so excited about the approach that she volunteered to come into the nursery each week, take stories from other children and lead the acting out. One year later and she is still at the setting on a voluntary basis.

Nurseries that are delivering Helicopter Stories and Helicopter at Home have found ways to share stories, passing books between home and school or including stories as part of the conversations they have with parents on a regular basis. Isla set up story-sharing boards in each school, where parents and teachers can post stories. Having a mutual understanding of the value placed on these is opening the way for greater relationships between families and settings.

Parents who have trained on Helicopter at Home comment that for many of them, this is the first time they have been in a classroom since they left school, and they remark how stimulating they find it to be learning in a positive playful environment.

> Helicopter at Home gives me a way to play with my child. Before this training I didn't know how to. I love listening to their stories and making up my own. How great to know that when I do, I'm helping them to learn.

Hospital Helicopter

Jennifer Lunn, theatre director and one of MakeBelieve Arts Creative Associates, has for a number of years been developing an adaption of Helicopter Stories in her work with children who are seriously ill.

As one of the storytellers for the Readathon in Hospitals charity, Jen visits children's wards around London with the purpose of sharing stories. Trained as a MakeBelieve Arts Helicopter Deliver, she became interested in how she could incorporate the benefits of Storytelling and Story Acting in her work with these children.

The age range of the children Jen works with runs from 3 to 16. Sitting at their bedside, she lets the children know that she is collecting stories and asks if they are happy to add to her collection, so that their story can be shared with other children in the hospital. She often reads the children stories she has been told and then asks if they are happy to dictate.

If a child is struggling to come up with a story, Jen uses Rory's story cubes to help her find a starting point. Many of the more seriously ill children are isolated from others of their age, and the dice act as a way to support them when there are no other peers around. The child roles the three cubes, which contain characters, objects and locations, and the pictures at the top of each die act as a stimulus.

Many of the children Jen works with are very ill, and she often finds herself asking questions to support the children in telling their story or to refocus them on the activity. Once it is finished, she reads the stories back, sometimes to an invited audience of parents and nurses.

Jennifer has also been trialling the benefits of running hospital story sessions with a group of actors, who join her to bring the children's stories to life. This works better when the children are on the ward rather than in individual rooms, and it does restrict the number of stories she is able to take. On the flip side, the enjoyment the children get from seeing their stories acted by adults offers another layer of validation to their words.

Whether the stories are acted, read to an audience or included in a collection to be shared with other children in the hospital, Jen believes this work is valuable at this difficult time in children's lives.

> In the same way as Helicopter Stories gives children confidence in their own voices, this process also gives a voice, and a degree of control, to children who have almost no

control at all over their own personal narrative, and so it can be empowering at a time when they really need it."

Jennifer Lunn, MakeBelieve Arts Creative Associate

The story that follows comes from Molly, a seven year-old who spends three days a week in hospital on a dialysis machine. She dictated this to Jen in June 2014 during one of her treatment days. The surgical metaphors of the story are striking. Jen has scribed hundreds of stories from children over the past few years and has noticed that many of the stories she takes from children who are seriously ill include contents around being trapped and then being rescued by their parents.

The scary shark

In the ocean lived a fish called Jen. She was swimming and then a shark came. Jen pulled a terrible face because she was trying to scare the shark but the shark ate her all up.

Inside the shark, Jen found a shark's tooth. She used the tooth to cut the shark open. The shark growled at her, but she was free and she swam back to her mother's house.

The mum saw the terrible shark with a cut open door in him and it was what Jen did. She said, 'Go away' to the shark, but the shark ate the mum up.

The mum found another shark's tooth in the shark's stomach, and she cut the shark open with it. Then she swam home to her husband.

The husband pulled a terrible face when he saw the shark, and he managed to scare the shark away and the shark never came back.

(Molly, age 7)

Looking at this story, it is easy to see the potential of this approach to help children to step outside their problems and for a short time change or take control of the outcome of their narrative.

Jen's work enables children who are in hospital to hear the stories of others, to appreciate the voices of children in similar situations and to know their story is listened to, even when they are seriously ill.

Jane Katch's fifth graders

A few years ago, I was privileged to visit Jane Katch's fifth-grade classroom and observe how she uses Storytelling and Story Acting as a way to evaluate and edit the stories of the class.

The tables in Jane's room are arranged in a horseshoe so that children can climb under them and have access to an acting space whenever it is needed. The day I was visiting, the group had just finished the first draft of their stories and were about to put them on their feet.

One by one Jane read out the stories, inviting members of the class to act them out. The authors didn't get involved, choosing instead to watch their stories unfold and see what was needed to make their narrative stronger. At the end the class discussed each story and suggested additional information they would have liked to give them a clearer picture.

In an e-mail, Jane told me, 'I had been trying to convince my students to value the process of revising their stories. Although they would do it because I insisted on it, they did not understand the intrinsic reason to revise until we began to act out their first drafts. As soon as they saw their stories acted out, revision became a meaningful part of the writing process. The authors now wanted their words to accurately tell the actors what to do and say, so when the actors were confused or the directions were not clear, the students would immediately make changes to their written stories'.

I was amazed at the sophistication of the group and how they valued the opportunity to act out their stories as part of the editing process. This made sense to me. If I want to understand something, I will often put it on its feet, reading it out loud or even moving around to help me find clarity. Seeing the benefits these young people took from sharing their work was incredible. Because their stories were acted out, they had a living representation of the images they were trying to convey. This helped them to appreciate how far they had come with their writing and also to realise what else they might need to do.

Onwards and upwards

As I reflect on all the different ways Storytelling and Story Acting can be used, it becomes clear to me how powerful an approach this is. It places story at the centre of children's learning and connects the narratives of their lives with the narrative of the classroom. It uses the tools of play to support children's engagement.

There are probably many other adaptions yet to be discovered. For something that in essence is so simple, I relish the opportunity to see how it grows.

Onwards and upwards . . .

Let's end on a story

Once upon a time a bird was flying around its nest.
And then it saw a tree what looked all shiny.
And the bird called his mum. And he told his mum he saw a shiny tree.
And his mum told him, 'There's no such thing as a shiny tree'.
And the bird said, 'Yes there is'.
And his mum came to look. And his mum saw the shiny tree, and she told him,
'Let's pick all the shiny leaves off'.
So they did.

(Jade, age 4)

When I heard this story I felt sad. I thought about it a lot. Why did the mum pick the leaves off the shiny tree? I asked this question to Jade and she said, 'Cos that's what she did'.

I thought some more, and I found myself thinking how we sometimes respond when children share their shiny trees with us. Maybe at first we deny it exists; we don't really want to see it, or we are too busy. But if the child persists and persuades us to look at the shiny tree, which might be a painting, or a model or even a piece of writing, then maybe we start to suggest things he could do to improve it. 'Perhaps you could paint the sky blue, or stick eyes on the front of the box, or change that word for a more descriptive one'. Gradually we pick the leaves from their shiny tree. It's no wonder I felt sad.

But then I thought positively about Helicopter Stories and about the world Vivian Gussin Paley has opened for so many children and adults, and I realised that this is an approach that values the shiny trees of us all.

So I hope you discover many shiny trees as you begin this work. Approach it with curiosity and care and share the joy that happens, when imaginations fly. . . .

Books by Vivian Gussin Paley

Bibliography

Publications

Boal, Augusto. (1979) *Theatre of the Oppressed*. New York: Theatre Communications Group.

Cooper, Patsy. (1993) *When Stories Come to School: Telling, Writing and Performing Stories in the Early Childhood Classroom*. New York Teachers and Writers Collaborative.

Cooper, Patsy. (2009) *The Classrooms All Young Children Need: Lessons in Teaching from Vivian Gussin Paley*. Chicago: University of Chicago Press.

Cremin, T., Swann, J., Flewitt, R., Faulkner, D., Kurcicova, N. (2013) Evaluation Report of Make-Believe Arts Helicopter Technique of Storytelling and Story Acting. Esmee Fairburn Foundation, December. www.*makebelievearts*.co.uk/s/*Helicopter*-Technique-*Evaluation*.pdf.

Dennett, Daniel. (1991) *Consciousness Explained*. Boston: Back Bay Books.

Egan, Kieran. (1986) *Teaching as Storytelling: An Alternative Approach to Teaching and Curriculum in the Elementary School*. Chicago: University of Chicago Press.

Gottschall, Jonathan. (2012) *The Storytelling Animal: How Stories Make Us Human*. New York: Mariner Books.

Haven, Kendal. (2007) *Story Proof: The Science behind the Startling Power of Story*. Westport, CT: Libraries Unlimited.

Holland, Penny. (2003) *We Don't Play with Guns Here: War and Weapon and Superhero Play in the Early Years*. Maidenhead: Open University Press.

Johnstone, Keith. (1989) *Impro: Improvisation and the Theatre*. London: Methuen Drama.

Katch, Jane. (2002) *Under Deadman's Skin: Discovering the Meaning of Children's Violent Play*. Boston: Beacon Press

Lee, Trisha. (2011) The Wisdom of Vivian Gussin Paley. In Linda Miller and Linda Pound, *Theories and Approaches to Learning in the Early Years*. London: Sage.

Paley, Vivian Gussin. (1986) On Listening to What Children Say. *Harvard Educational Review*, 56, no. 2.

Paley, Vivian Gussin. (1988) *Mollie Is Three: Growing Up in School*. Chicago: University of Chicago Press.

Paley, Vivian Gussin. (1990) *The Boy Who Would Be a Helicopter: The Uses of Storytelling in the Classroom*. Cambridge, MA: Harvard University Press.

Paley, Vivian Gussin. (1998) *The Girl with the Brown Crayon: How Children Use Story to Shape Their Lives*. Cambridge, MA: Harvard University Press.

Paley, Vivian Gussin. (2000) *White Teacher*. Cambridge, MA: Harvard University Press.

Paley, Vivian Gussin. (2004) *A Child's Work: The Importance of Fantasy Play*. Chicago: University of Chicago Press.

Pinker, Steven. (1994) *The Language Instinct*. London: Penguin.

Robinson, Ken. (2009) *The Element: How Finding Your Passion Changes Everything*. New York: Penguin Books.

Singer, Isaac B. (1989) *Naftali the Storyteller and His Horse*. London: Faber Children's Books.

Trevarthen, Colwyn. (2010) What Is It Like to Be a Person Who Knows Nothing? Defining the active intersubjective mind of a newborn human being. *Infant and Child Development*, 20, 119–135.

Wolf, Gary. (1996) Steve Jobs: The next insanely great thing. *Wired Magazine*. February.

Wood, D. J., Bruner, J. S., & Ross, G. (1976) The role of tutoring in problem solving. *Journal of Child Psychiatry and Psychology, 17*(2), 89–100.

Videos

Armstrong, David, and Matlock, Resa. (2001) *The Boy Who Could Tell Stories*. Ball State University Childcare Collection, Muncie, Indiana.

Online Videos

Boston Listens: The Wisdom of Vivian Paley. http://bpsearlychildhood.weebly.com/the-wisdom-of-vivian-paley-and-trish-lee.html.

Boston Listens: Videos about their programme. http://bpsearlychildhood.weebly.com/story telling.html.

Gilbert, Elizabeth. Ted Talk. www.ted.com/talks/elizabeth_gilbert_on_genius?language=en.

Lee, Trisha. Helicopter Stories Keynote https://youtu.be/38CXtfZULSg

Lee, Trisha. The Helicopter Technique of Storytelling and Story Acting. http://youtu.be/UkJl8dyzRQQ.

Online PDF Reports

Ellis, George, F. R. (2011) *Biology and Mechanisms Related to the Dawn of Language*. Cape Town: University of Cape Town. http://tinyurl.com/prx8v92.

National Advisory Committee on Creativity and Cultural Education. (1999) *All our Futures: Creativity, Culture and Education*. London. http://tinyurl.com/nmbm3g5.

Online Articles

Nicolescu, Basarab. (1990). Peter Brook and Traditional Thought. www.gurdjieff.org/nicolescu3.htm.

Paul, Annie Murphy. (2012) Your Brain on Fiction. *New York Times Sunday Review*. http://tinyurl.com/7ufgfnx.

Rich, Diane. (2003) Bang, Bang! Gun Play: And Why Children Need It. *Early Education Journal*. http://tinyurl.com/2aoomut.